ANTONÍN DVOŘÁK'S
New World Symphony

Oxford KEYNOTES
Series Editor　KEVIN BARTIG

Sergei Prokofiev's Alexander Nevsky
KEVIN BARTIG

Rodgers and Hammerstein's Carousel
TIM CARTER

Aaron Copland's Appalachian Spring
ANNEGRET FAUSER

Arlen and Harburg's Over the Rainbow
WALTER FRISCH

Arvo Pärt's Tabula Rasa
KEVIN C. KARNES

Beethoven's Symphony No. 9
ALEXANDER REHDING

Claude Debussy's Clair de Lune
GURMINDER KAUR BHOGAL

Brian Eno's Ambient 1: Music for Airports
JOHN T. LYSAKER

Alfred Schnittke's Concerto Grosso no. 1
PETER J. SCHMELZ

Jean Sibelius's Violin Concerto
TINA K. RAMNARINE

George Bizet's Carmen
NELLY FURMAN

Puccini's La Bohème
ALEXANDRA WILSON

Antonín Dvořák's New World Symphony
DOUGLAS W. SHADLE

Oxford KEYNOTES

ANTONÍN DVOŘÁK'S NEW WORLD SYMPHONY

DOUGLAS W. SHADLE

Oxford University Press is a department of the University of Oxford. It furthers
the University's objective of excellence in research, scholarship, and education
by publishing worldwide. Oxford is a registered trade mark of Oxford University
Press in the UK and certain other countries.

Published in the United States of America by Oxford University Press
198 Madison Avenue, New York, NY 10016, United States of America.

© Oxford University Press 2021

All rights reserved. No part of this publication may be reproduced, stored in
a retrieval system, or transmitted, in any form or by any means, without the
prior permission in writing of Oxford University Press, or as expressly permitted
by law, by license, or under terms agreed with the appropriate reproduction
rights organization. Inquiries concerning reproduction outside the scope of the
above should be sent to the Rights Department, Oxford University Press, at the
address above.

You must not circulate this work in any other form
and you must impose this same condition on any acquirer.

CIP data is on file at the Library of Congress
ISBN 978–0–19–064563–2 (pbk.)
ISBN 978–0–19–064562–5 (hbk.)

DOI: 10.1093/oso/9780190645625.001.0001

Series Editor's
INTRODUCTION

Oxford Keynotes reimagines the canons of Western music for the twenty-first century. With each of its volumes dedicated to a single composition or album, the series provides an informed, critical, and provocative companion to music as artwork and experience. Books in the series explore how works of music have engaged listeners, performers, artists, and others through history and in the present. They illuminate the roles of musicians and musics in shaping Western cultures and societies, and they seek to spark discussion of ongoing transitions in contemporary musical landscapes. Each approaches its key work in a unique way, tailored to the distinct opportunities that the work presents. Targeted at performers, curious listeners, and advanced undergraduates, volumes in the series are written by expert and engaging voices in their fields, and will therefore be of significant interest to scholars and critics as well.

In selecting titles for the series, Oxford Keynotes balances two ways of defining the canons of Western music: as lists of works that critics and scholars deem to have articulated key moments in the history of the art, and as lists of works that comprise the bulk of what consumers listen to, purchase, and perform today. Often, the two lists intersect, but the overlap is imperfect. While not neglecting the first, Oxford Keynotes gives considerable weight to the second. It confronts the musicological canon with the living repertoire of performance and recording in classical, popular, jazz, and other idioms. And it seeks to expand that living repertoire through the latest musicological research.

Kevin Bartig
Michigan State University

CONTENTS

ABOUT THE COMPANION WEBSITE   viii

ACKNOWLEDGMENTS   ix

ABBREVIATIONS   xiii

PROLOGUE: THE BIG PROBLEM   xv

1 The Welcome Arrival   1
2 The Symphonic Premiere   15
3 The Aesthetic Conflict   39
4 The National Question   53
5 The Brewing Storm   73
6 The Fiery Debate   91
7 The Racial Challenge   113
8 The Spiritual Aftermath   137

EPILOGUE: THE GREAT BEYOND   165

APPENDIX: THE MUSICAL TORNADO   171

SUGGESTED READING   175

INDEX   177

ABOUT THE COMPANION WEBSITE

www.oup.com/us/dvoraksnewworldsymphony

This book discusses a wide range of musical repertoire, from some of the world's most beloved pieces to those that stand outside our collective memory. To help readers orient their ears to the soundscapes of orchestral music from the period, the companion website contains playlists featuring the music performed on the concert programs introducing each chapter and selected pieces mentioned in the main text. Digesting this soundscape will enable readers to determine for themselves how they might have responded to the New World Symphony at its 1893 premiere.

ACKNOWLEDGMENTS

Thanks to a nudge from my friend Kevin Bartig, I floated the idea of this book to Kevin Karnes at the 2014 American Musicological Society meeting. Karnes was Oxford Keynotes editor at the time, and he worked with me closely to get the project off the ground, offering valuable advice from the start. In a pure coincidence, Bartig took over the Keynotes editorship as I was finishing. Both Kevins have been tremendous collaborators.

The Provost's Office at Vanderbilt University supported the project by awarding me a grant sponsored by the Southeastern Conference that allowed me to complete archival work on Florence Price at the University of Arkansas. Staff at the Mullins Library there—Timothy Nutt, Angela Fritz, and Geoffery Stark—helped me navigate the enormous mass of documents. Price scholars Jim Greeson and Barbara Garvey Jackson also offered invaluable support while I was in residence. Funds awarded through the Vanderbilt iSeminar program allowed me to hire Erika Ikizake and Sage Pope as student assistants to digitize materials in Atlanta and Chicago. I couldn't have completed the book without them.

I honed my arguments in several locations: the Midwest chapter and national meetings of the American Musicological Society, the North American Conference on Nineteenth-Century Music, Washington University in Saint Louis, the University of Amsterdam, and, of course, Twitter. I'm especially grateful to Todd Decker and Kasper van Kooten for invitations to speak at their institutions, and to all the listeners who've provided insightful feedback. Susan McClary offered especially enthusiastic support. Zachary Woolfe and Joshua Barone at the *New York Times* gave me space to share my thinking with their readership for the 125th anniversary of the New World Symphony's premiere in December 2018. Anne Midgette kindly amplified my findings in the *Washington Post* and has continued to share ideas about the piece with me.

Several friends and colleagues—Aubrey Bergauer, Kira Thurman, Kristen Turner, Will Gibbons, Katherine Preston, Will Robin, Samantha Ege, Jim Davis, Emily Richmond Pollock, Doug Bomberger, Lucy Caplan, Chris Bowen, and Gwynne Kuhner Brown—took an interest in the project and generously shared resources, ideas, or potential leads as they stumbled across them. My mentor Evan Bonds wrote right away when he heard the New World Symphony emerge out of nowhere in the film *O. J.: Made in America* and has continued to offer significant advice. Travis Stimeling and Will Gibbons are the best sounding boards a writer could ask for.

My Vanderbilt colleagues Joy Calico, Melanie Lowe, Jim Lovensheimer, Ryan Middagh, Josh McGuire, Emily Lordi,

Celia Applegate, Kim Welch, Emily Greble, and Frank Candelaria have all been a constant source of support, and I owe them for all the slow email responses it caused. The Blair School library staff—Holling Smith-Borne, Sara Manus, Jacob Schaub, and Michael Jones—came through for me countless times. Several other librarians and researchers worked heroically during the COVID-19 shutdown to help me acquire materials I couldn't access in person: Jon Silpayamanant (Indiana University Southeast), Benjamin Knysak (RIPM), Isabel Planton and Jody Mitchell (Indiana University Bloomington), Stefan Philipp (Bayerische Staatsbibliothek), Caroline White (University of Massachusetts), Bill Levay (New York Philharmonic), and Tom Lisanti (New York Public Library).

Suzanne Ryan at Oxford University Press helped me launch the project and supported it with her characteristic energy and fire. She stepped down from OUP partway through the process, but Norm Hirschy took up the mantle and has been a delight to work with. The peer reviewers for the press helped me find the appropriate contours for the book's argument and helped me find the right balance between narration and scholarly intervention. (Thanks, Pat!) Lucy Caplan (Harvard University) and Beth Stewart (Verismo Communications) read the entire manuscript prior to final submission and offered invaluable feedback on every facet of the book. They went above and beyond the call of duty while saving my writing from itself. Joe Matson provided keen copy edits. Shalini Balakrishnan and Arockia Rajan at Newgen expertly guided the production process, and I can't thank Rachel Lyon enough for creating another outstanding index. Leah Broad (University of Oxford) and

I spent a whirlwind afternoon working through the proofs together. I owe her some biscuits!

A final round of thanks goes to my family—Karen, Avery, and Cecily—for offering love and support while I finished this book during the global COVID-19 pandemic. My father, William Shadle, passed away before he could see it in print. It is dedicated to his memory and to my mother, Anne.

ABBREVIATIONS

FPPA	Florence Price Papers Addendum, Mullins Library, University of Arkansas
LSP	Lamar Stringfield Papers (3522), Southern Historical Collection, The Wilson Library, University of North Carolina at Chapel Hill
TTP	Theodore Thomas Papers, The Newberry Library, Chicago
DBP	W. E. B. Du Bois Papers (MS 312), Special Collections and University Archives, University of Massachusetts Amherst Libraries
AAJ	*American Art Journal*
BDE	*Brooklyn Daily Eagle*
BDA	*Boston Daily Advertiser*
BDG	*Boston Daily Globe*
BET	*Boston Evening Transcript*
BH	*Boston Herald*
ChiDef	*Chicago Defender*
ChiTr	*Chicago Tribune*
CinCG	*Cincinnati Commercial Gazette*

CinEn	*Cincinnati Enquirer*
CG	*Cleveland Gazette*
DIO	*Daily Inter Ocean*
DJM	*Dwight's Journal of Music*
Indep	*The Independent*
MT	*London Musical Times*
MW	*London Musical World*
MA	*Musical America*
MC	*Musical Courier*
MO	*Musical Observer*
MV	*The Musical Visitor*
NZfM	*Neue Zeitschrift für Musik*
NMR	*New Music Review*
NYEP	*New York Evening Post*
NYG	*New York Globe*
NYH	*New York Herald*
NYHE	*New York Herald*, European Edition
NYMWT	*New York Musical World & Times*
NYS	*New York Sun*
NYT	*New York Times*
NYTr	*New York Tribune*
NYW	*New York World*
WES	*Washington Evening Star*
WaPo	*Washington Post*
WAJ	*Watson's Art Journal*

PROLOGUE
THE BIG PROBLEM

Evan Bonds, my dissertation advisor, emailed me a few years ago to ask if I'd seen *O. J.: Made in America*, Ezra Edelman's Oscar-winning documentary about O. J. Simpson. I hadn't, but he said I needed to watch Part 4 right away. The film traces the escalation of racial tension in the United States that overlaid Simpson's storied football career and subsequent fall from grace. Sure. Why not? I'm always up for a good documentary.

Like many Americans, I remember watching Simpson's infamous Ford Bronco "chase" in 1994. Perhaps unlike many white Americans my age, I also vividly recall the exact moment of his acquittal. October 3, 1995: I was a ninth grader at Fuller Junior High—a school in Sweet Home, Arkansas, a predominantly Black neighborhood just outside the city limits of Little Rock. The city's torturous history of race relations had taken me there, because white students like me rode buses from other areas of town as part of longstanding desegregation initiatives. My biology teacher had stopped class to turn on the TV. "We the jury in the above-entitled action find the defendant Orenthal James Simpson not guilty of the crime of murder." Students poured out of classrooms, cheering, clapping, and shouting. Jubilance. That's what I remember.

It was also around ninth grade that I was introduced to Antonín Dvořák's New World Symphony, more formally known as his *Symphony No. 9, "From the New World."* I don't remember the exact circumstances, but I bought a recording and listened dozens of times while conducting an imaginary orchestra in my living room. Although I didn't have the vocabulary to describe the conventional four-movement structure of a symphony like this one, the drama across the entire piece shook me. The catchy melodies stuck with me. And something about it unleashed my imagination. Little did I know that it had caused a sensation at its 1893 New York premiere only to become a staple for orchestras around the world.

Edelman's hard-hitting documentary pushed the boundaries of my hearing over twenty years later. The film reaches a climax with Simpson's acquittal in Part 4. Prior to this moment, the soundtrack is an original score hovering in the background. But when the jury spokesperson starts reading the verdict, the haunting English horn solo from the second movement of the symphony slips into the sonic frame. As the gentle melody unfolds, the scene cuts to an interview with a pastor of a Black church in Los Angeles: "Free at last. Free at last," he said, recalling his feelings at the acquittal, "Thank God Almighty, he is free at last."

The music changes again a few seconds later. Other passages from the symphony—fast, buoyant sections—accompany a montage of period footage showing Black communities erupting in cheers after awaiting the verdict with bated breath. I suddenly felt like I was hearing the soundtrack to my own memory. The scene then shifts abruptly to forlorn groups of white people stunned by the outcome. They are cloaked in silence. For them, the music stops.

Edelman's provocative deployment of the symphony stunned me. I'd been researching this book for several months before I saw the film, but I immediately knew that a simple retelling of the symphony's premiere and reception wouldn't be enough. The opposing reactions to the Simpson verdict reminded me of the inflamed reactions to Dvořák's symphony after its premiere—responses that often coalesced around issues of race. In fact, the entire discourse surrounding Dvořák's tenure as director of the National Conservatory between 1892 and 1895 reflected the country's broader racial divides at the dawn of the Jim Crow era—a period marked by lynching, disenfranchisement, segregation, the conquest of Native American lands, and a continuous struggle for equality. The deep connections between the symphony, the film, and my own history made the music speak to me in a new way.

Why does this change of perspective matter? The typical concert hall experience is designed to remove music from the messiness of politics, as if it occupies a space outside time and lived history. But how can a piece of music so deeply entangled in racial politics ever be grasped with a frame that doesn't account for the exploitation of Black labor? The erasure of Black history? The relative absence of Black music and musicians in those very concert halls? This book argues that the New World Symphony crystallized the racialization of American classical music that has marked its history for nearly two centuries.

The first five chapters funnel toward the symphony's premiere while tracing specific issues that defined the stakes of Dvořák's US residency: professional music education, the critical reception of his music, instrumental music aesthetics, national musical identity, and how to construct an American musical style. Each chapter peels back a new layer that reveals how seemingly apolitical musical concerns quietly reinforced sharp divides between European American whiteness and African American Blackness, to say nothing of indigeneity or East Asian heritage—topics that often arose alongside the others in public life.

The story reaches a climax in chapter 6, when Dvořák's contention that Black vernacular music should form the basis of a distinctly American classical style launched a months-long debate riddled with racist invective that put the white racial foundation of American classical music on full display. Chapter 7 shows that Dvořák's presence became an inflection point for Black musicians resisting white cultural dominance, especially after the New World Symphony's premiere. Perhaps recalling the tragicomic sequence of events that followed O. J. Simpson's acquittal, such as the Kardashian family's rise to stardom, the final chapter sketches the far-reaching (and sometimes bizarre) ripple effects of Dvořák's residency on American musical culture.

To help pull readers into an appropriate musical landscape, each chapter begins with an imagined description of a historical concert that foreshadows the chapter's main themes. And fair warning: the cast of characters I've assembled—musicians, writers, politicians, and even Kim Jong-il—is extraordinarily long and diverse for a book this size. But to hear the symphony with new ears compels us to acknowledge many sides of its story that remain largely unheard. With that in mind, listening to it might make us more uncomfortable than we'd like. After writing this book, I know I'll never hear it the same way again.

CHAPTER 1

THE WELCOME ARRIVAL

October 21, 1892—New York City

With flowers adorning the lobby of Andrew Carnegie's new Music Hall on a crisp fall evening, eighty members of two rival orchestras, the Philharmonic Society and the Symphony Society, joined forces under the baton of Anton Seidl, one of the city's greatest musical celebrities, to give a New York welcome to a distinguished European guest.

At 8:15 p.m., three hundred choristers led by Richard Henry Warren, music director at St. Bart's Episcopal, launched into a rendition of the hymn "America," inspiring the packed house to rise to its feet and join at full volume.

Colonel Thomas Wentworth Higginson, the evening's venerable master of ceremonies, walked slowly onto the stage. Known as a fierce abolitionist and supporter of women's suffrage, he spoke for twenty impassioned minutes about the parallels between Christopher Columbus's journey to the New World and the installation of the evening's honored guest, Dr. Antonín Dvořák, as director of Jeannette Thurber's National Conservatory.

"The triumphs of our own land in music, like most of our artistic triumphs, lie in the future," Higginson closed with a flourish. "Let us hope that our guest of tonight may help add the new world of music to the continent which Columbus found." A tall order for one person.

"Speechmaking is altogether too common an offense," *Times* critic W. J. Henderson reported the next day, "and when it is so tenuous in thought, so platitudinous in style, and so lachrymose in delivery as the oration of the eminent Bostonian who spoke last night, it is altogether a weariness of the flesh. So much for the 'boom' part of last night's entertainment."[1]

    Little did Henderson know that Dvořák
    would change the course of American music
    forever.

Why all the hoopla for a conservatory director? The landscape of American higher education evolved rapidly after the Civil War. Scores of public land-grant colleges, private research universities, normal schools for teachers, and institutes devoted to African American students greatly expanded educational opportunities across the country. Professional music education also experienced a boom with the founding of private conservatories and university music schools. Although they offered professional training, the primary function of these schools was to supply the country with well-qualified music teachers—typically women, who enrolled at vastly higher rates than men. (Unlike their academic counterparts, many of the first music conservatories also admitted Black students.) Even so, thousands of aspiring musicians continued to travel to Europe for advanced musical training. Jeannette Thurber, a philanthropist of socially progressive causes (see figure 1.1), wanted to stem the tide in grand fashion.

Since studying at the renowned Paris Conservatory as a teenager in the 1860s, Thurber had dreamed of an institution in the United States that would be the envy of the musical world. Few people disagreed with the need, but how to fulfill it posed distinct challenges.[2]

The question arose at the highest levels of government as early as 1879. US Senator James Blaine, a Maine Republican,

FIGURE 1.1.   Jeannette Thurber. Courtesy Lilly Library, Indiana University.

thought a national conservatory was a good idea. "We are sadly in need of that," he argued on the Senate floor. "The Government of the United States does not do a single thing to encourage the cultivation of music. France gives eight million francs every year for this purpose in Paris. Why should we not do the same thing?" But he ultimately felt that the question stood outside the Senate's constitutional purview. Given the recent explosion of private conservatories, the idea of a federal institution also posed other political challenges. Senator Allen Thurman, an Ohio Democrat, said that he wouldn't want Cincinnati's "very fine conservatory," which had opened in 1867, crushed by the "power and purse of the National Government."[3]

Around the same time, a group of wealthy Black professionals in Brooklyn called the Lyric Swan Club established a different model in which students at an auxiliary music school would provide entertainment at club functions while learning practical skills on the fly. Unlike a traditional conservatory, students tended to be young working professionals barred from all-white organizations like the venerable New York Philharmonic and the new Metropolitan Opera Company. The school changed its name to the Mendelssohn School of Music in 1884 and soon began focusing almost exclusively on European classical repertoire from Beethoven to Wagner, thus offering students the opportunity to learn and perform in a variety of styles.[4]

Funded in part by her husband's grocery wholesaling fortune, Jeannette Thurber ultimately developed a similar entrepreneurial plan with Theodore Thomas, the country's most famous conductor. They wanted to establish an opera company tied to a conservatory that would supply it directly with well-trained musicians. Pitched as an alternative to the fledgling Metropolitan Opera Company, Thurber's two-part organization, the American Opera Company and the American Opera School, attracted a who's who of New York's philanthropists: Andrew Carnegie, Joseph Drexel, William Vanderbilt, and others seeking to display their noblesse oblige. The newly incorporated school's doors opened to a cohort of eighty-four students in September 1885.

With the school up and running, Thurber immediately reached higher. "As is well known," she told her backers at a Delmonico's lunch meeting a month later, "these institutions are established, or sustained, by the governments of all the principal countries of Europe. A prosperous and talented nation of 55,000,000 people certainly ought to be able to support an institution such as every petty State in Europe deems a necessity." This inspiring message hooked a nationwide network of supporters, including Henry Lee Higginson, founder of the Boston Symphony Orchestra (BSO) and a cousin of abolitionist Thomas Wentworth Higginson.[5]

Henry Higginson's endorsement signaled a broader reassessment of the performing arts and professional music education taking hold around the country. He had established the BSO four years earlier to be a "full and permanent orchestra, offering the best music at low prices." According to his plan, he would manage personnel and cover any deficits at the end of the season while the conductor would make all artistic decisions. This novel operational arrangement, unlike any other orchestra in the United States at the time, gave musicians stable employment and divorced artistic considerations from finances. Other ensembles needed to balance ticket sales carefully against costs, compelling them to take fewer artistic risks.[6]

Following Higginson's philosophy, Thurber wanted the conservatory to offer any student a world-class musical education regardless of background or ability to pay. To reach this goal, she requested an initial $100,000 from her board and sought annual infusions of $200,000 thereafter. And she truly wanted a broad base of national support. Her donors, she told the *New York Tribune* in 1885, already included "farmers and others whom you would think the last men in the world to care about supporting any artistic scheme."[7]

Meanwhile, Thurber's American Opera Company, which she intended to operate in a similar nonprofit arrangement, faced disaster. The company's lavish sets and costumes, coupled with Thomas's virtuosic orchestra and dozens of choristers and dancers, proved to be too expensive for her backers, who would have required the incentive of a financial return at that level of investment. Making matters worse, critics routinely complained about the weakness of the principal singers as well as the supposedly patriotic troupe's inappropriately foreign repertoire. A series of mishaps late in 1887 ultimately led to the company's demise, leaving the board holding massive debts. In the wake of this debacle, Thurber expanded the conservatory's curriculum and added all-star faculty members like pianists Rafael Joseffy and Adele Margulies, Metropolitan Opera principal cellist Victor Herbert, former Boston Symphony violinist Leopold Lichtenberg, and critics Henry Finck and James Huneker. The augmented faculty enabled students to pursue different tracks that could support a variety of musical goals, much like undergraduate music education in the twenty-first century.[8]

Fearing that the expensive conservatory would suffer the same fate as the opera company, Thurber and her board petitioned Congress for a $200,000 appropriation in February 1888. The petitioners argued that the school deserved the funds because it reached students from all over the country and provided an education at virtually no charge. Echoing her earlier sales pitch, Thurber added that "every European kingdom and republic" has a state-sponsored conservatory. "America has, so far, done nothing in a national way either to promote the musical education of its people or to develop any musical genius they may possess." Despite its high moral purpose, the petition proved to be politically untenable since people in small cities around the country would not want to support a national organization that didn't benefit them directly.[9]

Trouble was also brewing at the conservatory internally. Celebrated French baritone Jacques Bouhy, the inaugural director, resented Thurber's efforts to expand the curriculum and abruptly resigned in December 1888. Since the opera program comprised the core of the student body, dissolution seemed like a distinct possibility until Thurber announced that she was negotiating with acclaimed French composer Charles Gounod to take the post. While visiting Paris the following summer, however, she engaged another French baritone, Théophile-Adolphe Manoury, to lead the opera program, leaving the institution without a true executive director. If she wanted to secure the institution's long-term viability, a leader with a sound reputation was a virtual necessity.[10]

Thurber then targeted the nation's capital to gather momentum for the elusive congressional appropriation. To that end, she assumed management of Washington's new Lincoln Music Hall and engaged Higginson's Boston Symphony Orchestra and conservatory faculty for the venue's opening ceremony in December 1889. John W. Powell, an official in the US Geological Survey, quickly became her chief local advocate, and he was able to entice other luminaries like inventor Alexander Graham Bell and presidential advisor John Hay to donate to a scholarship endowment fund.[11]

Over the next several months, Thurber continued to stage events meant to attract locals with political clout. These efforts paid off when Commissioner of Education William Torrey Harris gave the conservatory a major endorsement in an open letter to the *Evening Star*:

> No one doubts that it is time for concerted action in this country to establish and endow a national conservatory of music that will take rank with the famous ones of Europe. Is it not equally obvious that it should be located in New York and that, as soon as may be, branches of the central institution should be established in other large cities of the country?[12]

To sustain the momentum, Thurber staged a concert exclusively featuring American composers at Lincoln Hall a few weeks later and proposed a similar festival in Omaha later in the year—a plan that received nationwide press coverage but never materialized.[13]

Thurber's scattershot approach to fundraising eventually moved in the right direction. Along with a group of backers from several states and the District of Columbia, she introduced a bill to Congress in December 1890 that would incorporate the conservatory under a national charter. Modifying Commissioner Harris's vision, they hoped to establish a central campus in Washington, transform the New York campus into a branch, and establish new branches in larger cities around the country. Remarkably, they did not request federal appropriations, opting instead to rely on private donations to feed the endowment. Congress approved the bill in March.[14]

With private fundraising for the scholarship endowment now a perpetual concern, Thurber needed more ideas for developing a broad base of support. Her next project involved building a Christopher Columbus Memorial in Washington that would house the new campus and open in spectacular fashion on the four-hundredth anniversary of the explorer's arrival. She also pursued the formation of a "national symphony orchestra" on the nonprofit model Higginson had devised for the Boston Symphony. Neither of these projects materialized. Unfailing creative spirit without true musical leadership could not carry the institution forward.[15]

In 1891, Thurber finally pursued a blue-chip executive director from Europe who would oversee the conservatory's entire musical operation. After arriving at two names—Jean Sibelius and Antonín Dvořák (see figure 1.2)—Thurber sought the counsel of Adele Margulies, a Vienna-trained member of the piano faculty, who convinced her to settle on Dvořák. Thurber opened negotiations in June by offering him a two-year appointment to direct the conservatory, teach orchestration and composition lessons, and lead a handful of performances, all for an annual salary of $15,000—far more than he received in his position at the Prague Conservatory. To sweeten the pot, she also relieved him from summer duties so he could focus on composition.

FIGURE 1.2.   Antonín Dvořák, ca. 1891. Courtesy New York Philharmonic Leon Levy Digital Archives.

While seeking advice from friends, Dvořák communicated with Thurber through his London publisher, who eventually convinced him to sign a few months later.[16]

But Thurber didn't rest on her laurels. Shortly after closing the deal with Dvořák in December 1891, she began planning a Columbus Day festival at the Metropolitan Opera House to welcome her new director and feature a world premiere from his pen. When the opera house's interior burned the following summer, the quick-witted Thurber offered to combine the Met's remaining assets with those of the conservatory and build a new facility so that she could realize her original plan for the school to feed a professional troupe. This effort failed, but the conservatory hummed along.[17]

By October 21, when the city welcomed Dvořák with a grand concert in Andrew Carnegie's Music Hall, the composer had arrived safely and settled into his new role. Players from the city's two major orchestras came together under the baton of Anton Seidl. Rebuilding the Metropolitan Opera House could wait. And Thurber got her Columbus-themed event after all. "The musical season may be said to have officially begun," a critic for the *New York Sun* wrote the next day. "It is a good thing for the country—at least the musical world—to have a man of Dvořák's caliber in our midst. America is certainly the gainer by his coming." But if Dvořák was supposed to be a new Christopher Columbus, as Thomas Higginson argued in his speech that night, who in the equation represented the Native Americans he brutalized and enslaved remained an open question.[18]

NOTES

1 "Dr. Dvořák Introduced," *NYT*, 22 Oct. 1892.
2 David F. Labaree, *A Perfect Mess: The Unlikely Ascendancy of American Higher Education* (Chicago: University of Chicago Press, 2017), 36–54.
3 *Congressional Record* (Washington, DC: Government Printing Office, 1879), 8:1230–33.
4 "The Lyric Swan Club to the Front," *NYG*, 20 Jan. 1883; "The Mendelssohn School of Music," *NYG*, 17 May 1884; "Men and Music," *New York Freeman*, 30

Oct. 1886; William J. Simmons, *Men of Mark: Eminent, Progressive, and Rising* (Cleveland, OH: Geo. M. Rewell, 1887), 451–53.
5   "An American School of Music," *AAJ*, 31 Oct. 1885, 20.
6   "The Boston Symphony Orchestra," *BH*, 30 Mar. 1881.
7   "A High Priestess of Opera," *NYTr*, 1 Nov. 1885.
8   Katherine K. Preston, *Opera for the People: English-Language Opera and Women Managers in Late 19th-Century America* (New York: Oxford University Press, 2017), 410–94; Emanuel Rubin, "Jeannette Meyers Thurber and the National Conservatory of Music," *American Music* 8 (1990): 299–301.
9   "In Aid of Music," *WaPo*, 19 Feb. 1888; "The New York Times," *Indianapolis Journal*, 25 Feb. 1888.
10 "Trouble in a Conservatory of Music," *NYTr*, 17 Dec. 1888; "M. Théophile Manoury Engaged," *NYT*, 27 Sep. 1889.
11 "Music for the Nation," *WaPo*, 20 Apr. 1890.
12 "Music as a Center of Art," *WES*, 26 Feb. 1890.
13 E. Douglas Bomberger, *"A Tidal Wave of Encouragement": American Composers' Concerts in the Gilded Age* (Westport, CT: Praeger, 2002), 166–68.
14 *Congressional Record* (Washington, DC: Government Printing Office, 1891), 22:3804, 22:3854.
15 "A Great Music Hall," *WES*, 6 May 1890; "Mrs. Jeannette Thurber," *AAJ*, 12 Sep. 1891, 345.
16 Stefan, "Two Who Remember Dvořák," *MA* 61 (1941): 25; John Clapham, "Dvořák's Musical Directorship in New York," *Music & Letters* 48 (1967): 40–45.
17 Merton Robert Aborn, "The Influence on American Culture of Dvořák's Sojourn in America" (PhD diss., Indiana University, 1965), 109–11; "Grand Opera in English," *NYH*, 28 Sep. 1892.
18 "Antonín Dvořák," *NYS*, 22 Oct. 1892.

CHAPTER 2
THE SYMPHONIC PREMIERE

December 16, 1893—New York City

Another day of cold rain couldn't keep Carnegie's Music Hall from filling up for the Philharmonic's second concert of the season. The lobby buzzed with chatter about Dvořák's new symphony.

The anticipation was palpable when Anton Seidl raised his baton for the evening's appetizer—selections from Mendelssohn's *Midsummer Night's Dream*. But the orchestra lumbered through these magical delicacies, leaving most of the audience disappointed.

The mood lifted when the young violinist Henri Marteau, fresh from his studies at the Paris Conservatory, strode confidently onto the stage for his second Philharmonic appearance. Musically mature beyond his years, the soloist brought dignity and heft to the Brahms violin concerto, which was far more suited to Seidl's gravitas on the podium.

Everyone knew what was coming next. The great critic Henry Krehbiel had written a detailed analysis of the symphonic score in the *Tribune*, while the morning *Herald* had given a vivid description of the previous day's matinee rehearsal, where the fashionable audience had reportedly cheered "like the most excitable Italianissimi in the world."[1]

And yet with this detailed knowledge at hand, what came next was still a surprise. Bizarre harmonies oozed out of Seidl's baton as he looked at the low strings, the French horn, and the winds in turn. Then a flash of lightning! A storm throughout the entire orchestra heaved and tugged before giving way to a lively bouncing, almost familiar tune in the flute. The inexorable pull to the movement's climactic close led the enraptured crowd to leap to its feet in wild applause.

After Seidl took a few cautious bows, he raised his baton again, this time drawing mystical, almost organ-like chords from the winds and brass to start the second movement. Then, as if floating on a cloud of lush strings, the English horn sang a tune that could make anyone cry. After the final dying repetition of this forlorn melody, the brass returned to their mystical chords, sending the violins to the stars.

"DVOŘÁK!" A single yell broke the fragile silence, but the crowd soon joined, "DVOŘÁK! DVOŘÁK!" until the composer stood, humbly acknowledged the applause, and soaked in what would be one of his greatest musical victories. After the audience settled to hear the rest of the symphony, the scherzo and finale whirled by like a tornado.

"We are inclined to regard it as the best of Dr. Dvořák's works in this form," critic W. J. Henderson wrote in the *Times*, "which is equivalent to saying that it is a great symphony and must take its place among the finest works in the form produced since the death of Beethoven."[2]

A little over a year after his arrival, Dvořák had indeed changed the American musical world (see figure 2.1).

Before Dvořák's arrival in 1892, Americans had every reason to believe that his position at the conservatory might enable him to elevate the international stature of

Philharmonic Society of New York

···FOUNDED 1842···
FIFTY-SECOND SEASON, 1893-1894.
ANTON SEIDL, - - - - CONDUCTOR.

Second Public Rehearsal, Friday, Dec. 15th, 1893,
AT 2 P. M.

Second Concert, Saturday, December 16th, 1893,
AT 8.15 P. M.

MUSIC HALL, 7th Avenue and 57th Street.

Soloist, - - - - Mr. HENRI MARTEAU.

— PROGRAMME: —
PART I.

Music to Shakespeare's "Midsummer Night's Dream," - MENDELSSOHN
a) Overture. *b)* Scherzo. *c)* Notturno.

Concerto for Violin, D major, op. 77. - - - - - BRAHMS
Mr. HENRI MARTEAU.
(Cadenza by Henri Marteau.)

PART II.
By Special Arrangement with the Composer,

FIRST PERFORMANCE
— OF —

Dr. Antonin Dvorak's New Symphony, E minor, No. 5 :
"FROM THE NEW WORLD."
(MANUSCRIPT.)

Box Office open daily from 9 A. M., to 5 P. M.

Prices for Reserved Seats : Parquet, $2.00 ; Dress Circle, first two rows, $1.50 ; Other rows, $1.25 ; Balcony, first two rows, $1 ; Other rows, 75 cents ; General Admission, $1 ; Boxes containing six seats, for Rehearsal, $12, for Concert, $15.

FIGURE 2.1 Program of New World Symphony Premiere, 16 Dec. 1893.
Courtesy New York Philharmonic Leon Levy Digital Archives.

the country's classical music culture. Competition with Europe had spurred the growth of the American conservatory system, as well as the acceleration of private funding for professional ensembles. Dvořák himself also seemed to epitomize the American dream. He had grown up in humble circumstances but had leveraged a tireless work ethic to reach nearly unmatched musical heights throughout Europe. Yet most people could not have expected that the racial landscape under Jim Crow might remind him of his ethnic marginalization in the German-speaking lands of Europe.

New York audiences first heard Dvořák's orchestral music in autumn 1879, when the entrepreneurial conductors Theodore Thomas, Leopold Damrosch, and Gotthold Carlberg scrambled to scoop the others (see figures 2.2 and 2.3). Thomas claimed victory in October, when he opened his season with a newly published Slavonic Dance. Writing for the *New York Tribune*, the distinguished critic John Hassard described it as a "composition of considerable strength and originality, full of pomp and splendor, and betraying the characteristic national taste for a semi-barbaric magnificence." Not letting New York take much of a lead, Bernhard Listemann and the Boston Philharmonic played four more of the dances in November and December. But the competition was far from over as conductors went on to premiere Dvořák's three Slavonic Rhapsodies and continued to program these pieces into the winter of 1880.[3]

The speed and intensity with which organizations tackled Dvořák's music reflected broader currents in the international marketplace. Johannes Brahms had recommended Dvořák's *Moravian Duets* to Berlin publisher Fritz Simrock in 1877. Hoping to turn a quick profit, Simrock commissioned a series of Slavonic Dances for four-hand piano in the vein of Brahms's Hungarian Dances from 1869. The immediate

FIGURE 2.2 Cartoon of Theodore Thomas in Cincinnati (1878). Courtesy Music Division, New York Public Library for the Performing Arts.

success of these new pieces cemented a long-term publishing relationship. Commercial availability then allowed Dvořák's music to travel through international distribution channels, which included the high-profile New York music shop operated by Gustav Schirmer, Leopold Damrosch's chief supplier. The tendency of US periodicals to translate or republish European essays and reviews only increased the public's appetite for both piano arrangements and full orchestral versions of his music.[4]

FIGURE 2.3. Leopold and Walter Damrosch. Courtesy New York Philharmonic Leon Levy Digital Archives.

Dvořák's rapid rise to popularity in the United States accompanied growing American interest in music that projected an Eastern European or Scandinavian folk ethos (see table 2.1). Critics often considered these pieces a welcome contrast to the German symphonic repertoire. A New York correspondent to *Dwight's Journal of Music*, for example, observed that Dvořák's second Slavonic Rhapsody

TABLE 2.1 "Eastern European" Orchestral Music in the United States, ca. 1878–1880

DATE	COMPOSER, WORK	ORCHESTRA, CONDUCTOR
December 5/7, 1878	Mikhail Glinka, *Kamarinskaya*	Symphony Society (New York), Leopold Damrosch
December 5/7, 1878	Johan Svendsen, Variations on a Norwegian Folktune, Op. 31	Symphony Society (New York), Leopold Damrosch
February 8, 1879	Piotr Ilych Tchaikovsky, Symphony No. 3, "Polish"	New York Philharmonic, Adolph Neuendorff
February 23, 1879	Johan Svendsen, Norwegian Rhapsody No. 4, Op. 22	Chickering Hall (New York), Gotthold Carlberg
February 23, 1879	Franz Liszt, Hungarian Fantasy, S. 123	Chickering Hall (New York), Gotthold Carlberg
October 6, 1879	Antonín Dvořák, Slavonic Dance in F, Op. 46, no. 4	Theodore Thomas Orchestra (New York)
October 6, 1879	Franz Liszt, Hungarian Fantasy, S. 123	Theodore Thomas Orchestra (New York)
November 7, 1879	Antonín Dvořák, Slavonic Dances in A and D, Op. 46, nos. 5 and 6	Boston Philharmonic, Bernhard Listemann
December 5, 1879	Antonín Dvořák, Slavonic Dances in C Minor and G Minor, Op. 46, nos. 7 and 8	Boston Philharmonic, Bernhard Listemann

TABLE 2.1 *Continued*

DATE	COMPOSER, WORK	ORCHESTRA, CONDUCTOR
February 4, 1880	Antonín Dvořák, Slavonic Rhapsody No. 3	Theodore Thomas Orchestra (Cincinnati)
February 21, 1880	Antonín Dvořák, Slavonic Rhapsody No. 1	Peabody Orchestra (Baltimore), Asger Hamerik
March 13, 1880	Antonín Dvořák, Slavonic Rhapsody No. 2	Symphony Society (New York), Leopold Damrosch
March 16, 1880	Antonín Dvořák, Slavonic Rhapsody No. 3	Brooklyn Philharmonic, Theodore Thomas
April 12, 1880	Antonín Dvořák, Slavonic Rhapsody No. 3	Theodore Thomas Orchestra (New York City)

"possesses a certain wild freedom, and even lawlessness that makes it very attractive" but "one could sober down by the aid of Beethoven, who can scarcely be deemed wild." Yet conductors had to be careful not to overdo it, as Hassard warned in his review of the same concert. "The Slavonic Rhapsody is full of beauty and originality," he noted, "but it was destroyed last night by a certain similarity in spirit to [Karl Goldmark's] *Penthesilea* overture."[5]

The sudden widespread availability of enticing works in a variety of genres helped Dvořák make a strong first impression in the early 1880s, but a lasting place on orchestral programs was far from secure. On the one hand, well over a dozen pieces by older composers like Joachim Raff and Anton Rubinstein had already become perennial favorites.

On the other, composers closer in age to Dvořák, including Edvard Grieg and Max Bruch, produced a steady stream of new material that attracted premiere-hungry conductors. The key to the first group's staying power was success with one or more symphonies.

Unfortunately for Dvořák, the symphonic field was also crowded. Mature composers like Brahms and Boston's John Knowles Paine had written two well-received symphonies in recent years. Among musicians of Dvořák's generation, Frederic Hymen Cowen, an emerging star in London, eagerly sought a place beside them. After Theodore Thomas and the New York Philharmonic performed Cowen's Third Symphony in November 1882, critic John Hassard felt that "it ought to assure his position in the front rank of the contemporary English school." Leopold Damrosch, meanwhile, had taken it on a Western tour, where an enraptured critic in Louisville described it as "the fitful breath of summer leaves that whisper the secrets of dreamland, or the soft drone of bees that hum of the charms of Hyblaea."[6]

Dvořák kept pace with his Sixth Symphony when Theodore Thomas premiered it in New York only two months after Cowen's. At the Philharmonic's public rehearsal, the typically drowsy afternoon audience, "not inclined to be demonstrative," gave it rowdy applause. After the concert the next night, one enthusiastic critic called it "the most solidly and impressively scored [symphony] we have had in a long time, in which respect it bears a close resemblance to Brahms's best works." The piece thrilled Boston audiences later in the year, sending Dvořák well on his way to a more permanent place on American orchestral programs.[7]

TABLE 2.2 Dvořák's Orchestral "Competition" in New York, 1881–1885

COMPOSER/WORKS	DATE	ORCHESTRA, CONDUCTOR
Johannes Brahms		
Symphony No. 1	November 6, 1880	SSNY, L. Damrosch
Symphony No. 2	April 9, 1881	NYP, T. Thomas
Academic Fest. Overture	November 3, 1881	SSNY, L. Damrosch
	November 19, 1881	BPS, T. Thomas
Tragic Overture	November 12, 1881	NYP, T. Thomas
Haydn Variations	February 16, 1884	NYP, T. Thomas
	March 1, 1884	BPS, T. Thomas
Symphony No. 3	November 15, 1884	NYP, T. Thomas
Hans Bronsart		
Frühlings-Fantasie	January 8, 1881	SSNY, L. Damrosch
Anton Bruckner		
Symphony No. 3	December 5, 1885	SSNY, W. Damrosch
Frederic Hymen Cowen		
Symphony No. 3	November 11, 1882	NYP, T. Thomas
	February 16, 1884	NYP, T. Thomas
	March 1, 1884	BPS, T. Thomas
Symphony No. 4	April 11, 1885	NYP, T. Thomas
Felix Draeseke		
Symphony No. 2	May 2, 1885	SSNY, W. Damrosch
Antonín Dvořák		
Symphony No. 6	January 6, 1883	NYP, T. Thomas
Hussite Overture	November 15, 1884	NYP, T. Thomas
Scherzo Capriccioso	November 8, 1884	BPS, T. Thoms
	November 14, 1885	NYP, T. Thomas
Symphony No. 7	January 9, 1886	NYP, T. Thomas
Robert Fuchs		
Serenade No. 1	February 3, 1883	BPS, T. Thomas
Symphony No. 1	December 10, 1885	TTO, T. Thomas

Continued

TABLE 2.2 *Continued*

COMPOSER/WORKS	DATE	ORCHESTRA, CONDUCTOR
Hermann Grädener		
Capriccio	January 6, 1883	NYP, T. Thomas
Hans Huber		
Symphony No. 1	February 11, 1882	NYP, T. Thomas
Alexander Mackenzie		
Scotch Fantasy, *Burns*	November 3, 1883	BPS, T. Thomas
Jean-Louis Nicodé		
Symphonic Variations	January 10, 1885	NYP, T. Thomas
John Knowles Paine		
Symphony No. 2	March 31, 1883	BPS, T. Thomas
The Tempest	November 20, 1884	BPS, T. Thomas
Joachim Raff		
Symphony No. 3	December 9, 1882	NYP, T. Thomas
	February 7, 1885	BPS, T. Thomas
Symphony No. 5	February 9, 1884	SSNY, L. Damrosch
	February 14, 1885	NYP, T. Thomas
Symphony No. 8	November 7, 1885	SSNY, W. Damrosch
Hugo Reinhold		
Concert Overture	February 10, 1883	NYP, T. Thomas
Prelude, Minuet, & Fugue	February 14, 1885	NYP, T. Thomas
Anton Rubinstein		
Symphony No. 5	December 10, 1881	NYP, T. Thomas
Symphony No. 2	February 4, 1882	SSNY, L. Damrosch
	April 7, 1883	NYP, T. Thomas
La Russie	December 16, 1882	SSNY, L. Damrosch
Symphony No. 4	January 19, 1884	NYP, T. Thomas
Fantasia eroica	April 18, 1885	BPS, T. Thomas
Camille Saint-Säens		
Suite Algérienne	April 23, 1881	BPS, T. Thomas
Xaver Schwarenka		

TABLE 2.2 Continued

COMPOSER/WORKS	DATE	ORCHESTRA, CONDUCTOR
Symphony in C Minor	December 12, 1885	NYP, T. Thomas
Charles Villiers Stanford		
Serenade in G Major	January 19, 1884	NYP, T. Thomas
Richard Strauss		
Symphony No. 2	December 13, 1884	NYP, T. Thomas
Johan Svendsen		
Romeo and Juliet	March 12, 1881	NYP, T. Thomas
Piotr Ilych Tchaikovsky		
Symphony No. 2	December 8, 1883	SSNY, L. Damrosch
Serenade for Strings	January 24, 1885	SSNY, L. Damrosch

Heightened by new commissions from London's Royal Philharmonic Society, the brewing symphonic rivalry between Cowen and Dvořák pressed into subsequent seasons. But both of their next efforts fell flat in New York. After hearing Cowen's Fourth, W. J. Henderson of the *Times* wrote, "Mr. Cowen, in truth, belongs to the rank and file of learned musicians who have mastered the technique of their art, but, having power of speech, have unluckily, nothing to say." The *Tribune*'s new critic, Henry Krehbiel, also found little substance in Dvořák's Seventh. "It was listened to respectfully, applauded courteously, and that was all," he observed. "It did not conquer the right to a permanent place in the local concert repertory."[8]

The tepid response to these two symphonies reflected a larger sea change in New York's critical makeup in the mid-1880s. Critics of Hassard's generation, including those who wrote for predominantly African American newspapers, typically served an educational function by providing accessible descriptions of new pieces and taut evaluations of performances. Henderson and Krehbiel, in contrast, brought aesthetic agendas to the profession that moved well beyond education. Both men, as well as James Huneker of the *Musical Courier* and Henry Finck of the *New York Evening Post*, leaned heavily toward the searing emotional depth and sensuous coloration of Richard Wagner's music. Henderson, for example, described Johannes Brahms's Third Symphony as "absolutely devoid of aught but the interest attaching to a mosaic of tones," adding, "the sooner it is shelved the better." Writing a well-constructed, enjoyable piece was no longer enough to earn the younger critical establishment's support.[9]

AN ENDURING PRESENCE

Despite the lukewarm reactions, Dvořák's commercial reach and gift for speedy writing enabled his works to remain on programs around the country. Between 1884 and 1887, ensembles in Boston and New York gave US premieres of around a dozen new works. His shorter character pieces also continued to be attractive contrasts to established Germanic repertoire. A Boston critic swooned over the *Scherzo Capriccioso*, for example, remarking, "there are phrases that go like laughter, like contention, like rivalry, like good companionship."[10]

His symphonies, on the other hand, continued to underwhelm. After a Boston Symphony performance in Washington, DC, a local critic called the Seventh "tame compared with the unapproachable scoring of the great

German master"—Richard Wagner. W. J. Henderson rejected the Sixth, describing the adagio as "utterly lacking in inspiration" and the finale as "on the whole not a striking piece of writing." Krehbiel coolly dismissed the Fifth after its New York premiere: "It has been neglected hitherto, we should say, because it deserved to be neglected."[11]

The uneven responses to Dvořák's music in the United States belied his steadily rising reputation abroad, especially in Britain. The London premiere of his Stabat Mater in spring 1883 moved him into the forefront of the British musical imagination after auspicious performances of his Sixth Symphony a year earlier. A critic for the *Musical Times* felt that the new choral work "approaches as near to greatness as possible, if it be not actually destined to rank among world-renowned masterpieces." Dvořák's journey to Britain in 1884 helped create a pathway toward lasting fame. A writer for the *London Standard* explained, "While example after example of his skill was presented to metropolitan amateurs, it remained for the advent of the musician himself to place the crowning seal upon his popularity."[12]

Though Dvořák's presence was perhaps unnecessary for his star to rise, his British reputation continued to flourish as he visited the country seven more times before relocating to the United States in 1892. After hearing him conduct his Seventh Symphony, an entranced London critic dubbed it "one of the greatest works of its class produced in the present generation." His choral works became fixtures after he conducted them at festivals in Birmingham and Leeds. The London premiere of his Eighth Symphony, facilitated by none other than Frederic Hymen Cowen, incited the audience to call him to the stage three times. And an honorary doctorate from Cambridge University, awarded in June 1891, was a signature recognition.[13]

Given the history of polarized responses to Dvořák's music in the United States, celebrity status in Britain still didn't make him the most obvious choice to direct Thurber's conservatory. She very well might have selected Cowen, who had become director of the prestigious Royal Philharmonic Society in 1888, Hans Richter, easily one of the most famous conductors in London and Vienna, or even Piotr Ilyich Tchaikovsky, who had visited the United States for the opening of Carnegie's Music Hall in May 1891. But one of the earliest biographical sketches of Dvořák published in the United States proved that he had a firsthand grasp of the value of educational philanthropy, Thurber's central aim for the conservatory:

> His wealth of ideas clamored for expression, but he had not enjoyed instruction in composition, and his small earnings could not gain him access to symphony and chamber music concerts. It was even denied him to look at the score of the works performed here, to say nothing of possessing them. Finally, he found a friend in Carl Bendl, who at once opened to him all the treasures of his musical library.[14]

A personal testimony published in a London newspaper that circulated widely in US magazines revealed that he was also likely to sympathize with her patriotic mission. "Every child in Bohemia must study music," he said. "Herein, I consider, lies one great secret of the natural talent for music in my country. Our national tunes and chorales come, as it were, from the very heart of the people, and beautiful things they are." Only Dvořák seemed to offer the right combination of musical achievement, popular celebrity, and personal background to be Thurber's ideal partner in her philanthropic enterprise.[15]

HEARING THE NEW DIRECTOR

The music-loving public was naturally curious about what Dvořák might accomplish during his residency. Biographical sketches, interviews, and a heavy dose of speculation percolated through the press as early as September 1891, well before he signed his final contract. "It is at best a hazardous experiment," a jealous writer for the *Chicago Tribune* warned, "and New York should not count its chickens before they are hatched." Henry Krehbiel expressed grave doubts about the entire prospect, surmising that Dvořák had fallen into "the vice of writing too much, which has been so injurious to the fame of Raff and Rubinstein." Hopeful that his inspiration wouldn't dry up by the time he arrived, Americans had two more opportunities to hear his latest works before he started his new post.[16]

The US premiere of his Requiem split critics down the middle. Henry Finck, a member of the conservatory faculty, called the piece a "masterwork of its kind," assuring readers that Dvořák's presence would be "a matter for supreme satisfaction." Joining him, W. J. Henderson dubbed it a "masterly work" that "teems with original ideas," noting the "wonderful manner in which Dvořák has made use of Slavonic harmony and tone-coloring." Krehbiel, who might have been inclined to appreciate this national touch, felt the piece "looks better [on the printed page] than it sounds" and "becomes monotonous before the mass is half-finished."

Another critic found it "devoid of spontaneous musical beauty, too bizarre and too national in themes, and dry, and elaborately factitious in his treatment, dull and prolix in too great preponderance for its success." This sharp division did not bode well for Thurber, at least if critics reflected broad public sentiment. What if Dvořák was a flop?[17]

The Eighth Symphony offered critics one more opportunity to imagine the country's impending musical future. And what they heard left as many questions as it answered:

> BOSTON MUSICAL HERALD: Sticklers for conventional forms might reasonably object that it was rather a suite of tone-pictures than a symphony; but why should we care for names, or be so narrow as to demand everlastingly that the new should conform to the old? Let us have the new wine in new bottles. Let us welcome, if we can, the wealth of invention, the splendor of tone-coloring, the vivacity of spontaneous creation—even though it has a touch of barbaric opulence and wildness—which characterized this new work.[18]

> BOSTON EVENING TRANSCRIPT: Of Dvořák's new symphony we can, with the best will in the world, find nothing good to say. No one can damn a work after a single hearing; but we mistake much if this one will not be found to have damned itself. To perform it, as a composition in an important form by a composer of Dvořák's prestige, was eminently proper; we doubt, however, if Mr. Nikisch or any member of the orchestra will care to look at it again. One is tempted to say, as a French critic once said of a certain requiem, "Brought out at its own funeral!"[19]

> NEW YORK EVENING POST: Dvořák's new symphony is one more leaf in the laurel crown of the great Bohemian, who is soon to be a New Yorker. There is less of the national element

in it than in some of his earlier works, and the Bohemian is evidently becoming more and more cosmopolitan.²⁰

THE INDEPENDENT (NY): It is a short rather than a long symphony, highly condensed in its impetuous working up, and with a few departures from formal models. Of these the most noticeable to the popular listener is an impassioned slow waltz instead of a scherzo, after the license of Tschaikowsky—for one other modernist and nonconformist in symphonies.²¹

AMERICAN ART JOURNAL (NY): There is no great depth or transcendent height attained in the Symphony, but it is beautiful, melodic and symmetrical, and the harmony, as usual with Dvořák, assumes new and attractive forms without undue straining for effect. [. . .] The more we hear of Dvořák's compositions the more we congratulate ourselves and the public on the fact of his pending residence in New York, due to the enterprise and art spirit of Mrs. Jeannette M. Thurber, director of the National Conservatory.²²

This kaleidoscope of opinions revealed that critics wanted to find *something* they could envision as a hopeful direction for the future—classicism, modernism, lightness, depth, national color, or cosmopolitanism. And so they did. (Well, most of them.) The broader public of music lovers could feel assured that a composer bearing such widespread criticism would soon make the United States his home.

For her part, Thurber had continued to set her sights on opera. As early as October 1891, Dvořák had warmed to the idea of a uniquely American opera. By January, magazines were reporting that he "proposes to write an opera to an American libretto if he can find one suitable." To test his mettle, Thurber asked him to write an American-themed cantata for his welcome concert in October 1892, but they settled on a Te Deum instead. Although Thomas Wentworth Higginson's fiery speech proclaiming Dvořák a musical Christopher Columbus had primed the audience for greatness, most listeners left the hall underwhelmed by the music. "No one finds fault with a woman of moderate means when she tempers her August robe to meet the November blast," one critic wrote, "but on the contrary praises her skill. When an eminent composer, however, makes a—shall we say it?—hash of some of his old ideas and dresses it with a *sauce piquante* of orchestration, we always grumble."[23]

Thurber continued to press Dvořák on the prospect of an opera and gave him Henry Longfellow's *Song of Hiawatha* to spark his imagination. But an eclectic variety of individuals introduced Dvořák to the music of Black Americans soon after his arrival. Most directly, a Black voice student at the conservatory named Harry T. Burleigh frequently sang spirituals in the director's home, leaving a distinctly positive impression on him. One of only a handful of Black students, Burleigh also assisted Dvořák with various administrative tasks and was "at the head of his classes," according to his friend Harry Smith, editor of the *Cleveland Gazette*. By February 1893, at least one prominent magazine had reported that "Dr. Dvořák is putting the finishing touches on his [Ninth] Symphony. At present the composer is studying the peculiarities of our Southern negro music which he finds very interesting and seems to possess in its intervals some relation to Slavic melodies." Something interesting was on the horizon.[24]

In May 1893, just before Dvořák planned to leave New York with his family for the summer, the *Herald* published an explosive interview. "I am now satisfied," he said, "that the future music of this country must be founded upon what are called negro melodies. This must be the real foundation of any serious and original school of composition to be developed in the United States." While he visited the Bohemian enclave of Spillville, Iowa, and made side trips to Nebraska, Minnesota, and the World's Fair in Chicago, the musical world roared with debate about his sweeping comments. His new symphony, which Anton Seidl and the New York Philharmonic agreed to premiere in December, was supposed to prove his hypothesis.[25]

The day before the premiere, the *Tribune* ran an extensive description of the symphony replete with musical examples critic Henry Krehbiel had gleaned from the manuscript score. "A pervasive element in African music." "Distinctively negro characteristic." "The story of Hiawatha's wooing." "Strongly suggestive of Beethoven and Schubert." The *Herald* ran an interview with the composer on the same day: "I therefore carefully studied a certain number of Indian melodies which a friend gave me," he said, "and became thoroughly imbued with their characteristics—with their spirit, in fact." Listeners were clearly in for something unusual, because Dvořák had turned squarely toward non-European sources for inspiration in a quintessentially white European genre.[26]

NOTES

1 "Dr. Dvořák's American Symphony," *NYTr*, 15 Dec. 1892; "Dr. Dvořák's Great Symphony," *NYH*, 16 Dec. 1892.
2 "Dr. Dvořák's Latest Work," *NYT*, 17 Dec. 1892.

3 "The Thomas Concert," *NYTr*, 7 Oct. 1879; "Musical," *BET*, 8 Nov. 1879; "Stage and Concert Hall," *BDG*, 6 Dec. 1879.
4 David Brodbeck, *Defining Deutschtum: Political Ideology, German Identity, and Music-Critical Discourse in Liberal Vienna* (New York: Oxford University Press, 2014), 143–46; "Music in Vienna," *Musical Review*, 11 Dec. 1879, 141–42.
5 "Musical Correspondence," *DJM*, 27 Mar. 1880, 55; "The Symphony Society," *NYTr*, 14 Mar. 1880.
6 "The New-York Philharmonic Concert," *NYTr*, 12 Nov. 1882; "The Damrosch Concert," *Louisville Courier-Journal*, 23 Nov. 1882.
7 "The Philharmonic Society," *NYT*, 6 Jan. 1883; "The Philharmonic Society," *NYTr*, 7 Jan. 1883; "Music," *Indep*, 11 Jan. 1883, 9; Proteus, "Boston Notes," *MV*, Dec. 1883, 324.
8 "The Philharmonic," *NYT*, 12 Apr. 1885; "The Philharmonic Society," *NYTr*, 10 Jan. 1886.
9 "Philharmonic Rehearsal," *NYT*, 5 Nov. 1884; Horowitz, *Moral Fire*, 77–78.
10 Ticknor, "The Symphony," *BDG*, 29 Jan. 1888.
11 "Amusements," *WaPo*, 12 Jan. 1888; "The Philharmonic Society," *NYT*, 10 Mar. 1888; "The Symphony Society," *NYTr*, 13 Dec. 1890.
12 "Richter Concerts," *The Standard*, 17 May 1882; "Stabat Mater," *MT*, 1 Mar. 1883, 156; "Herr Dvořák," *The Standard*, 24 Mar. 1884.
13 "This Week," *Athenaeum*, 2 May 1885, 575; Viktor Fischl, "Dvořák in England," *Proceedings of the Musical Association* 68 (1941–42): 1–17; John Clapham, "Dvořák and the Philharmonic," *Music & Letters* 39 (1958): 126–27; "Dr. Dvořák at Cambridge," *MT*, 1 July 1891, 409.
14 "The Life of Anton Dvořák," *AAJ*, 21 July 1883, 245.
15 "Music and Art," *Christian Union*, 23 Feb. 1888, 250; "Dvořák," *MV*, Apr. 1888, 92; "Music in Bohemia," *AAJ*, 19 May 1888, 67.
16 "New York Gets Dvořák," *ChiTr*, 13 Sep. 1891; "Musical Comment," *NYTr*, 3 Nov. 1891.
17 "Dvořák's Requiem," *NYEP*, 26 Feb. 1892; "Church Choral Society," *NYT*, 26 Feb. 1892; "Dvořák's Mass for the Dead," *NYTr*, 26 Feb. 1892; Stevenson, "Music," *Indep*, 3 Mar. 1892, 13
18 "Music in Boston," *BMH*, Apr. 1892, 92.
19 Apthorp, "Boston Symphony Orchestra," *BET*, 29 Feb. 1892.
20 Finck, "Recent Concerts," *NYEP*, 14 Mar. 1892.
21 Stevenson, "Music," *Indep*, 17 Mar. 1892, 9.
22 Thoms, "Seidl Brings Out Two Novelties at the Philharmonic," *AAJ*, 19 Mar. 1892, 498.
23 "How Dvořák Conducts," *ChiTr*, 4 Oct. 1891; "Dvořák and his American Engagement," *MV*, Jan. 1892, 10; "Antonín Dvořák," *The Critic*, 29 Oct. 1892, 236.

24 Thurber, "Dvořák as I Knew Him," *The Etude*, Nov. 1919, 693; "In New York City," *CG*, 19 Nov. 1892; "Dr. Dvořák," *AAJ*, 4 Feb. 1893, 327; Michael Beckerman, *New Worlds of Dvořák: Searching in America for the Composer's Inner Life* (New York: W. W. Norton, 2003), 79–98 and 126–30.
25 "Real Value of Negro Melodies," *NYH*, 21 May 1893; "Musical Matters," *NYTr*, 15 Nov. 1893.
26 "Dr. Dvořák's American Symphony," *NYTr*, 15 Dec. 1893; "Dvořák on his New Work," *NYH*, 15 Dec. 1893.

CHAPTER 3
THE AESTHETIC CONFLICT

December 17, 1892—New York City

Carnegie's Music Hall hummed with excitement as the crowd gathered to hear *two* special guests making their debuts with the orchestra: Dr. Dvořák conducting his D major symphony and pianist Ferruccio Busoni, lately of Boston's New England Conservatory.

At 8:00 p.m., the genial Anton Seidl strode on stage and, with a glance, set the kettledrums rolling to start Karl Goldmark's passionate overture on the Prometheus myth. The maestro suddenly began moving as if controlled by marionette strings, pulling voluptuous melodies and a rainbow of colors from the orchestra and revealing every emotional nuance of the tragic tale.

Warm applause greeted the young Italian pianist (and his long, wavy hair), known here only as a chamber musician. His restrained temperament at the keyboard and fidelity to Beethoven's score suited the sparkling Fourth Piano Concerto. The appreciative audience was moved to call for an encore, and he obliged with Liszt's "La Campanella"—a magic trick for the fingers.

A series of four sea pictures by Belgian composer Paul Gilson, the only new piece of the evening, stretched Seidl and his orchestra to their physical limits. The rolling of waves at dawn, a sailor's dance, a love duet between English horn and flute, and at last a heaving storm that opens to glorious, brassy sunshine—was it a dream?

Waiting for Dvořák's arrival, a few listeners glanced at the program notes written by Arthur Mees: "It no longer admits of any doubt that Dvořák is one of the greatest of living composers. He is an apostle of absolute music. His compositions are not the result of a reflection or of an effort to translate given thoughts into tones. Everything that impresses him turns of itself into music. He lives in a tone world."

Suddenly the Bohemian appeared on stage, acknowledging the applause with his characteristic humility. In the first two movements of his Sixth Symphony, he was quiet on the podium, almost reserved, with his left hand at his side. But a fire erupted inside him during the third movement, a Bohemian furiant, a characteristic national dance. The orchestra responded in equal measure. The sweeping melodies of the finale roused the tired audience after a long evening of intense music, leaving Dvořák with a soft smile.

"After music like that of M. Gilson," Henry Krehbiel observed in his review, "Dvořák's symphony brings solace."[1]

Dvořák's near universal popularity in the United States by the time he arrived in September 1892 obscured the fact that his music also stood at the center of a raging conflict about the nature of music itself. Adherents of "absolute music" believed that music followed its own aesthetic logic revealed in purely instrumental genres. Others argued that music should be more closely connected to the real world—emotionally, sensually, politically. These groups hated each other. But, through their very denial of music's political resonance, the American adherents of absolute music betrayed a deep investment in white European cultural dominance since it conveniently allowed them to overlook the realities of racial politics.

Throughout the nineteenth century, a preference for abstract instrumental music often signaled a sense of intellectual superiority—that a listener had the mental capacity to comprehend this otherworldly realm or that a composer hadn't stooped to the level of making a piece's meaning glaringly obvious. In 1846, for example, Boston critic John Sullivan Dwight attacked the vivid musical narratives of local composer Anthony Philip Heinrich on moral grounds: "We are sorry to see such circumstances dragged into music as the 'Indian War Council,' the 'Advance of the Americans,' the 'Skirmish,' and 'Fall of Tecumseh,'" he wrote, whereas "music, aiming at no subject,—music composed with no consciousness of anything in the world *but* music, is sure to tell of greater things than these."[2]

In that same year, 1846, German composer Richard Wagner coined the term "absolute music" to describe the ideal that Dwight was seeking. But Wagner thought purely instrumental music was an irrelevant abstraction, *not* an ideal. As did Heinrich. "Mr. Dwight is a happy wight," he wrote in a letter to a friend, "for he lives in serene solitude at Brookfarm among the chirpings of some innocent insects, and the Concertos of Bullfrogs, the latter like the symphonies of Beethoven needing no programmes, speaking for themselves to the mind of that contemplative gentleman." Both Heinrich and Wagner thought music could be—and should be—something more than *just* music.[3]

Contentious debates about the nature of music intensified after the 1853 premiere of New York composer

William Henry Fry's *Santa Claus: Christmas Symphony*. Critic Richard Storrs Willis dismissed it as an "extravaganza" unworthy of serious analysis, prompting an angry Fry to explain his philosophy:

> What is music, let me ask, in defining my position as a composer? Is it learning, or mathematical intricacies? No: if it be only those, I would leave off writing and take up mathematics where I left, and learn to calculate an eclipse. Is it imitating classical models? No: it is the original mode of expressing an original idea.[4]

In other words, is music absolute? No. Despite being wordless, he thought, music could be a medium for conveying concrete ideas. Pulling politics into the equation, Fry elaborated that his musical opponents were just as naïve as those who "trust in religion, in government, and in political economy all things which bear the sanction of ages." And perhaps proving the point, Willis told Fry that the composer was "making a parrot of that which is a nightingale—a wretched tone-*slave* out of what is a glorious tone-*master*." (Fry, incidentally, would write a major antislavery treatise in 1860.)[5]

Later in 1854, leading Viennese critic Eduard Hanslick would echo Willis's position in his famous treatise *On the Musically Beautiful* by describing the "content" of music as music itself. Like Fry, progressive German-speaking composers Peter Cornelius and Franz Liszt retorted that the idea of absolute music was not only musically empty but politically reactionary. Using the metaphor of enslavement, Cornelius sought to "renounce" the false freedom of absolute music and the "bondage" of established classical forms. Liszt coined a term of his own to describe pieces created with these goals in mind: "program music." A program in this case wasn't a sheet of paper distributed before a concert, but a political or philosophical program.[6]

News about the budding conflict between the Hanslick and Liszt camps reached American shores almost immediately through Liszt's piano student William Mason, which caused it to escalate in the United States. As with Fry's *Santa Claus*, Liszt's "music of the future" encountered staunch resistance from US critics who didn't understand it and rejected its potential political resonance (see figure 3.1). After an 1857 two-piano performance of Liszt's symphonic poem *Les préludes* in Boston, for example, the conservative John Sullivan Dwight recoiled in horror: "We must have been very stupid listeners; but we felt after it as if we had been stoned, and beaten, and trampled underfoot, and in all ways evilly treated." Negative reactions to Liszt's symphonic poems also frequently took on a moralizing tone:

> The first offense is to take from music its own divine utterance, and to put in its place literalism, which is materialism; the second is to substitute violent color for simplicity of tone, abandoning the effects of melody for those of harmony, and leading the ear captive by splendid exaggerations. This is not the creative faculty which Beethoven had, (with what marvelous simplicity of means!) but the work of man's hands assured of death only, and not of immortality.[7]

Undeterred by this bewilderment and negativity, New York–based conductors continued to schedule these works on multiple programs per season throughout the

FIGURE 3.1. Music of the Future: Liszt's Symphonic Poems (1869). Courtesy Music Division, New York Public Library for the Performing Arts.

1860s and 1870s. And Anton Seidl would program Liszt's *Tasso* at Dvořák's welcome concert in October 1892.⁸

WAGNER RISING

Richard Wagner entered the American musical imagination at roughly the same time, partly because of his close affiliation with Liszt. But Wagner's aesthetic philosophy diverged significantly from Liszt's. Instead of program music, he argued that the *Gesamtkunstwerk*, a type of artistically integrated opera, should be the forward-looking alternative to absolute music.⁹

Beginning in the early 1850s, critic John Sullivan Dwight translated and reprinted several excerpts from Wagner's recent essays on opera and politics, introducing these new ideas to the English-speaking US public for the first time. Charles Callahan Perkins, a Boston-born composer living in Leipzig, wrote to warn Dwight that his feelings about Wagner had passed "from ardent curiosity, through aversion, to a firm conviction of the falseness" of his operatic theories. "If this music does succeed in forcing itself into admiration," Perkins wrote, "true Art would at least for a season die and disappear. I have this settled conviction that music in Germany is travelling fast on towards the regions of chaos." From Perkins's vantage, Wagner, Liszt, Robert Schumann, and the young Johannes Brahms were the "modern" composers leading the charge, whereas Ignaz Moscheles, Moritz Hauptmann, Niels Gade, and Ernst Richter ardently resisted.¹⁰

Aesthetic disputes about Wagner's theories, colored by moral posturing, continued unabated for years. In a sweeping, thirty-page review of Wagner's *Gesammelte Schriften* (1872), Boston composer John Knowles Paine observed that "it would be difficult to find any parallel to the present musical struggle, with respect to the acrimony and intolerance displayed by the disputants, the universality of the discussion, and the importance which the movement has for the future." Drawing heavily from the ideas of Austrian composer August Wilhelm Ambros, Paine hoped to forge a middle path that would keep the Wagnerian camp's positive innovations in orchestration while discarding the "degeneracy" of their "revolutionary" approach to form.[11]

But the battle lines remained firm. A New York audience "rose to their feet and shouted" after Theodore Thomas conducted Wagner's "Ride of the Valkyries" for the first time in September 1872. Reflecting on Thomas's efforts, critic Richard Grant White wrote that the only thing worse than sitting through a series of Wagner's operas would be "a series of symphonies by Liszt." On the other side sat John Van Cleve of Cincinnati, who couldn't get enough Wagner. "We listen to his operas," he mused, "and we revel in narcotic dreams, our sensations have always been intense; not always pleasurable; the roof has echoed, the air has trembled, and we have been agitated, we have been overpowered, and perforce stretched upon a bed, but it was the bed of Montezuma, and, though bright and red, was it a bed of roses?" Wagner wasn't going anywhere.[12]

Since permanent opera companies were virtually nonexistent in the United States before the Metropolitan Opera opened in 1883, Wagner's music reached a relatively broad national public primarily through orchestras and bands. Ongoing discussions about "the Wagner school" or "modern Germany" therefore penetrated deeply into the reception of new orchestral music. Throughout the 1870s, critics routinely evaluated symphonies by Joachim Raff, Anton Rubinstein, George Frederick Bristow, Johannes Brahms, John Knowles Paine, and others through the lens of their perceived affinity to Beethoven and Mendelssohn or Liszt and Wagner. Those that seemed to strike the right balance—Raff's Third and Rubinstein's Second, for example—remained relatively stable fixtures on concert programs over the next two decades.[13]

THE SYMPHONY OF THE FUTURE

Dvořák's Sixth Symphony hit US shores in the middle of this raging conflict. But before Americans had a chance to hear it, at least one London critic had primed the pump by firmly staking a claim for the anti-Wagner camp:

> The symphony of Dvořák is of the family of Haydn, Mozart, Schubert, and Beethoven. Dvořák, with Mendelssohn, Schumann, and Brahms, effectually controverts the dictum of Wagner, who declared the Beethoven had said the last word in absolute music. The last word! Heaven forbid. May Dvořák give us many more such discourses in absolute music as his Symphony in D, and add thereby proofs, other than the thousand already registered, of the fallibility of the harsh-tongued censor of Bayreuth.[14]

Although US critics tended to be less explicit when describing new works, several agreed with this assessment. John Hassard felt that Dvořák had "frankly accepted and respected the limits" of symphonic form. "Within them," he added, "a charming fancy plays freely, guided by knowledge and helped by the mastery of means of expression; a fancy exuberant, abundant, rich, so spontaneous and flowing, and of such strength and spirit, that is evident the reservoir is not yet exhausted." In other words, Dvořák hadn't succumbed to Wagnerism—and that was a strength.[15]

But William Thoms, the widely respected editor of the *American Art Journal*, disagreed. "Where is the happy consecutiveness of the old masters," he asked, "the smoothly-flowing harmonious music of Beethoven, who considered one grand climax in a composition quite enough?" Dvořák "was one of the most promising young musicians of the day," he continued, "but always prone to abruptness and startling changes. Instead of modifying this disposition the spirit of the times has led him to rather cultivate this defect than to moderate it." According to Thoms, Dvořák *had* succumbed to Wagnerism—and that was a weakness![16]

Throughout the last two decades of the century, variations on "dreariness" (absolute music) or "bluster" (Wagnerism) became the most consistent weapons in a critic's arsenal to signal the relative worth of a piece, regardless of the composer's intention. Henry Krehbiel, for example, found Dvořák's Seventh Symphony "too deficient in vital sentiment and too oblivious to the achievements of the last quarter century to take a hold upon the interest of the public." Even those who are "disposed to look favorably on each new effort to enrich symphonic literature," he continued, "will be put to it to find an argument to urge in favor of placing a work so weak in character as this among the best symphonies of the last decade." For Krehbiel,

Dvořák hadn't succumbed to Wagnerism—and that was a weakness.[17]

Perhaps in a direct response to Krehbiel, the arch-Wagnerian Finck evaluated the exact same music differently. "Herr Dvořák has evidently attended more than one Wagner 'cyclus' in Vienna," he noted enthusiastically, "and this symphony shows that he is rapidly becoming a disciple of Wagner not only by the character of its modulations, but by several distinct reminiscences of *Siegfried*, *Walküre*, and *Meistersinger*. In the scherzo there is also a suggestion of Raff's 'Lenore' symphony. Perhaps Dvořák cannot help being carried along by the Wagnerian maelstrom which at present is engulfing the whole musical world." According to Finck, Dvořák *had* succumbed to Wagnerism—and that was a good thing![18]

The sheer quantity and variety of Dvořák's music had allowed him to become an eminently malleable figure. On the one hand, it had the potential to unite critics on all sides of the aesthetic spectrum under a single banner. Listening to three separate performances of the symphonic variations in 1888, for example, critics in Chicago, New York, and Brooklyn, including the Wagnerians Krehbiel and Huneker, gushed that the piece was a tour de force of compositional prowess. On the other hand, Dvořák's music could evidently suit any aesthetic agenda. And Arthur Mees, the New York Philharmonic annotator, could call him an "apostle of absolute music"—someone who supposedly transcends politics—without anyone batting an eye.[19]

NOTES

1. "New York Philharmonic Society," *AAJ*, 24 Dec. 1892, 241; "The Philharmonic Society," *NYTr*, 17 Dec. 1892.
2. "'Father Heinrich' in Boston," *Harbinger*, 4 July 1846, 58–59.
3. Mark Evan Bonds, *Absolute Music: The History of an Idea* (New York: Oxford University Press, 2014), 1–2; Douglas W. Shadle, *Orchestrating the Nation: The Nineteenth-Century American Symphonic Enterprise* (New York: Oxford University Press, 2016), 54.
4. "A Letter from Mr. Fry," *NYMWT*, 21 Jan. 1854, 30.
5. Ibid., 29; "Reply to Mr. Fry," *NYMWT*, 28 Jan. 1854, 38.
6. Lee Rothfarb and Christoph Landerer, *Eduard Hanslick's On the Musically Beautiful: A New Translation* (New York: Oxford University Press, 2018), 41; Cornelius, "Concertmusik," *NZfM* 41 (8 Dec. 1854): 259 (my translation); Liszt, "Berlioz und seine Haroldsymphonie." *NZfM* 43 (1855): 25–32, 37–46, 49–55, 77–84, and 89–97.
7. Quoted in "Liszt's *Tasso*," *DJM*, 7 Apr. 1860, 11.
8. Mason, "Liszt and the Modern Music of Germany," *Musical Gazette*, 18 Nov. 1854, 9–10; "Concerts of the Week," *DJM*, 31 Jan. 1857, 143.
9. Bonds, *Absolute Music*, 129–40.
10. "Our Wagnerism," *DJM*, 21 Jan. 1854, 125.
11. Paine, "The New German School of Music," *North American Review*, Apr. 1873, 217–45.
12. "An Evening of Wagner," *NYTr*, 18 Sep 1872; White, "Franz Liszt," *Galaxy*, Sep. 1874, 390; Van Cleve, "Richard Wagner and His Art Problems," *Ladies' Repository*, Dec. 1875, 536.
13. Shadle, *Orchestrating the Nation*, 168–71.
14. Gwffyn, "Dvořák's Symphony," *MW*, 20 May 1882, 303.
15. "The Philharmonic Society," *NYTr*, 7 Jan. 1883.
16. "Philharmonic Society," *AAJ*, 13 Jan. 1883, 225.
17. "The Philharmonic Society," *NYTr*, 10 Jan. 1886.
18. "Third Philharmonic Concert," *NYEP*, 11 Jan. 1886.
19. "The Summer Night Concerts," *ChiTr*, 22 July 1888; "The Philharmonic Society's Concert," *NYTr*, 18 Nov. 1888; "The Philharmonic Society," *MC*, 21 Nov. 1888, 359; "Philharmonic Concert," *BDE*, 22 Dec. 1888.

CHAPTER 4
THE NATIONAL QUESTION

November 16, 1894—New York City

Although a construction accident had caused quite a stir at Carnegie's Music Hall the previous day, crowds thronged to hear the American debut of the "Champion of the Violin," Eugène Ysaÿe, and Dr. Dvořák's American symphony, back by popular demand.

Herr Seidl strode onto the stage with confidence, feeling the energy that had been brewing since the previous day's rehearsal. The familiar, intoxicating sounds of Karl Goldmark's *Sakuntala* flowed from the stage like honey until the final rousing climax sent the audience into thunderous applause.

An audible gasp rippled through the crowd as the Belgian violinist marched onto the stage with unmatched authority. With hands nearly as large as the violin itself, he looked as if he were shaping Saint-Saëns's ravishing Third Concerto like Michelangelo worked marble in his studio. His powerful sound filled every corner of the hall, overwhelming the audience with its majesty.

When Ysaÿe returned to the stage for Bruch's Scottish Fantasy, the orchestra's rendition of a Bach fugue faded like a distant memory, and his complete mastery over the violin once again penetrated the soul of every listener. After an awestruck pause—"Bravo!!" Shouts and thunderous applause compelled him to return to the stage for a final showpiece, a trifling etude by Lauterbach that became an object of reverence in his hands.

As the orchestra settled for Dvořák's thrilling symphony, listeners lucky enough to find a program, which were in short supply, took a moment to read Arthur Mees's comments: "Regardless of whatever traces of American national music so called may be found in it, the symphony as a musical creation pure and simple is of the highest interest. Spontaneous and vigorous in conception and masterly in every detail of construction it cannot but appeal to everyone musically receptive, of whatever nationality he may be." Under Seidl's supple direction, no one in the house could disagree.

"It is such a beautiful work and so replete with suggestion," William Thoms wrote in his review for the *American Art Journal*, "that it should be produced at every available opportunity."[1]

The premiere of Dvořák's New World Symphony would spark a fresh round of debate about American musical identity—what it meant, what it might sound like, and who had the authority to create it. Given the prominence of ongoing disputes about the "music of the future," however, questions about the nation were deeply intertwined with those about aesthetics. Can absolute music have a national identity at all? For someone like Arthur Mees, who believed that a work with clear national resonance like the New World Symphony could be "a musical creation pure and simple," the question was irrelevant: absolute music is universal.

Of course, nineteenth-century conceptions of national musical identity arose within the broader context of European and Russian imperialism. As imperial powers colonized broad regions of the Americas, Africa, and Asia, they often believed that Western "civilization"—laws, technologies, religious beliefs, and so on—constituted the universal pinnacle of human achievement and would enlighten supposedly "barbaric" non-European peoples. At the same time, various cultural groups *within* an empire—both at the center and on the peripheries—constructed national identities distinct from the imperial state in order to assert greater political and cultural autonomy. Universalist and nationalist ideologies sat in an uneasy tension across the Western world.[2]

What is a national *musical* identity, then? Nineteenth-century Western thinkers tended to believe that a "national spirit," or fixed national identity, somehow resides inside music. Of course, *how* this spirit, or essence, could become infused in music in the first place raises significant questions about compositional agency. Is the infusion a natural or an intentional process, or perhaps both? Influenced by ideas developed in Scotland and the German-speaking lands in the later 1700s, many nineteenth-century thinkers argued that the infusion process begins naturally as nations develop a collective anonymous repertoire of folksongs. Even in the United States, where people of diverse national and racial backgrounds lived together, writers tended to agree that a collective national spirit might emerge at some point in the future and animate a widespread national song repertoire.[3]

From this perspective, the collective anonymity of folksongs contrasted with the equally salient notion of "scientific music," or music reflecting the cultivation of an individual musical mind. In the later eighteenth century and into the nineteenth, philosophers considered scientific music an artificial creation distinct from "natural" folksongs. It became the musical equivalent of the civilizing empire. With the increasing publication of folksongs in notated formats, however, the distinction between "scientific" and "folk" music began to blur dramatically. The material object of the score became an authoritative version of a folksong capable of exact reproduction in performance, thus giving it the patina of civilized universality despite its supposedly national and "natural" origins.[4]

With folksongs now available to serve as raw musical material for compositional manipulation, composers developed several approaches to synthesizing this material with "scientific" techniques. The works arising from these various approaches became "art music"—a paradoxical concept meant to subsume the individual and the national, the past and the present, and the singular and the universal, into a transcendent musical whole. Indeed, well before "absolute music" became a governing concept after the 1850s, the concept of art music manifested the uneasy political tensions animating the European imperial apparatus.[5]

ART MUSIC IN THE UNITED STATES

The culturally and racially diverse population of the antebellum United States militated against the rapid development of a widespread anonymous folksong repertoire, at least according to the "natural" process theorized at the time. Americans of white European origin could claim cultural ties to the music of their European national ancestry, while these same individuals considered the music of Native Americans, enslaved Africans, and Asian immigrants "barbaric," and therefore un-American. At the same time, blackface minstrel troupes and their white musical suppliers like Stephen Foster used the system of copyright law to exploit the music of these same groups, especially enslaved

Africans, by repackaging them for white consumption on stage and in sheet music. In other words, white musicians used nonwhite "folk" repertoires that took root in the United States as tools for enriching themselves in the commercial marketplace.[6]

For these reasons, early US composers did not feel tied to vernacular traditions when writing instrumental music. Instead, they "clothed" what they perceived as a nonracial or nonethnic national essence in an eclectic variety of musical styles unrelated to folksongs. Composers Anthony Philip Heinrich and William Henry Fry, for example, used descriptive titles (and occasionally prose narratives) to signal a work's affiliation with a national theme. Heinrich's *The Ornithological Combat of Kings* (1847), which depicts birds from North and South America, and Fry's *Niagara Symphony* (1854) followed this approach. Fry also wrote music that diverged from conventional European forms and could be comprehended easily by average people, thus hopefully imbuing it with an American democratic spirit rather than a specifically folkish essence.[7]

Other US composers, including George Frederick Bristow and John Knowles Paine, simply continued writing music using the stylistic lingua franca of the German symphonic tradition—the musical analogue of "civilized" white European cultural superiority. From their perspective, the United States was a cultural extension of Western Europe rather than a distinct cultural unit, and their own identities as American-born musicians imbued any music they wrote with a national essence, regardless of style. One writer, Quebecois composer Calixa Lavallée, even argued that Boston composer Louis Maas's obviously Lisztian symphony, *On the Prairies*, could signal an American style precisely *because* the United States did not have "any musical tradition that would give a peculiar color."[8]

As European instrumental music rooted plainly in folksong or national dance gained popularity in the 1870s and 1880s, critics placed these pieces somewhere between absolute music and Wagnerism on the aesthetic spectrum. In their responses to Dvořák's Sixth Symphony, for example, nearly every reviewer described the furiant movement with phrases bordering on moralistic anti-Wagnerian invective: "eccentric rhythms," "full of tuneless shocks of sound, blarings, and drummings," "very odd, eager, and exciting," "unbridled impetuosity," "furiously wild," and "fierce."[9]

Even the typically judicious William Thoms of the *American Art Journal*, who had supported aesthetically progressive American composers like Bristow and Maas, derided national expression in Dvořák's symphony with a heavy dose of anti-Wagnerian invective:

> The popularity of the Slavonic style of music is as yet on the increase rather than on the wane, and anything that bears the name of a composer belonging to the Hungarian, Swedish, or Russian races is eagerly sought after, in the hope of discovering some extraordinary beauties that will astonish the blasé. In this manner many inferior works that are unworthy of a hearing are foisted upon the public, who, seeing nothing in them but a display of eccentricity and distorted harmonical combinations, are fain to believe this crudeness genius, and startling effects that make a true musician cringe as if from a blow are applauded because of that very series of sensational effects, that, if one would stop to reflect for a moment, is not music.[10]

By equating folk music with uncivilized noise, critics like Thoms signaled that aspiring American composers should *not* use Dvořák's methods of constructing a national identity if they wanted to maintain high artistic standards. To do so would be "uncivilized."

TRANSCENDING THE NATION

Dvořák himself was already no stranger to the sharp reactions these compositional methods could provoke. After Hans Richter conducted the Vienna premiere of Dvořák's Third Slavonic Rhapsody in 1879, the audience responded with a notable lack of enthusiasm. Political tension between the city's German and Czech residents had been on the rise and soon bubbled over when legal reforms benefitting Czechs sparked a surge in German nationalism. This anti-Czech sentiment contributed to a years-long delay of the Sixth Symphony's Vienna premiere despite its clear stylistic affinities with Brahms's Second. After the work's eventual premiere in 1883, a sympathetic Hanslick remarked that the third movement rose to the heights of purely musical beauty *despite* its ties to folk dance—precisely the opposite of William Thoms's earlier response in New York. For Hanslick, Dvořák had transcended the nation into the universal realm of absolute music.[11]

The notion that symphonic music could somehow transcend the nation was, paradoxically, an expression of nationalist sentiment in the German-speaking lands. Earlier in the century, many critics had perceived the timbral diversity and polyphonic texture of the symphony as metaphors of cosmopolitan cooperation—the individual uniting with the whole. At the same time, German critics and listeners claimed the symphony as a distinctly German genre, both in origin and in its essential musical qualities. From Hanslick's perspective, Dvořák's adoption of the German symphonic lingua franca had subsumed any traces of his Czech identity, no matter how overt, into a cosmopolitan German musical and political ideal.[12]

Meanwhile, critics in Britain and the United States embraced the cosmopolitan metaphor of the symphony but understood it as a mode of *universal* expression, thus purging it of German national resonance. Even so, the widespread acceptance of German historical superiority in symphonic composition—Haydn, Mozart, Beethoven, Mendelssohn, and Schumann were all culturally German, after all—solidified German musical and cultural dominance in these English-speaking countries. In the United States, the high percentage of German-speaking orchestral musicians and conductors, the wide circulation of German music periodicals, and the prominence of American musicians educated in German conservatories only reinforced this dominance well into the twentieth century. How to write a symphony that adequately addressed all aesthetic and national questions became one of the most salient compositional challenges for all non-German symphonists during the latter third of the nineteenth century. One British critic remarked that these composers "are put to a severe test when the form they have chosen [i.e., the symphony] precludes the prominent introduction of the national element, and when they are therefore thrown back on their unaided resources."[13]

Frederick Corder, a progressive British composer and pro-Wagnerian critic, outlined a strategy for passing this "severe test" in a remarkable 1885 essay called "The Future of the Symphony." Attempting to alleviate lingering fear that the symphony as a genre might be exhausted, he offered hopeful signs for the future and named Dvořák the only "legitimate successor of Beethoven and Schumann." And it was Dvořák's effective deployment of a national musical spirit that set him apart from others:

> Raff, Rubinstein, and most of the smaller fry among modern composers seem rather to have followed Mendelssohn's lead than Schumann's, and without any novel result. Dvořák alone, though he, too, like Brahms, has sought to keep in the Beethoven school, has been able to bring a distinct new element into the Symphony. In these days one is too apt to forget that the original Haydn Symphony was only a welding of the short Volkslied and Dance rhythms of four, six, or eight bars into a continuous and enlarged form. A more reverent regard for these Tunes, which are the soul of all music, would give our modern symphonies that vitality and interest which they so sorely lack. If Dvořák has not learnt this lesson it has come to him by instinct through the blood of his nation.[14]

Corder went on to argue that Lisztian thematic transformation, Wagnerian leitmotifs, or other formal experiments would destroy the unique character of the symphony and that *only* reclaiming connections to folk music would rejuvenate it—an elegant stylistic solution that was far from the norm in US critical paradigms.

Other British writers quickly followed suit when Dvořák's Seventh Symphony premiered later in the year.

"The great feature of the symphony," wrote the relatively conservative James Bennett, "is its frank assertion of origin. The music could have been composed by no man outside the composer's nationality, and within it, by no man save Antonín Dvořák." A reviewer for *The Athenaeum*, a literary magazine, agreed:

> Dvořák's music is equally interesting, and we may add satisfying, to adherents of the conservative and the progressive schools of art—to the former because it illustrates the fact that it is possible to create something entirely new and original without departing from the formal outlines or the canons of art laid down by the great masters of the past; to the more modern school because of the boldness of his harmonic progressions and the freedom of his rhythmic combinations. It has often been remarked that the Slavonic element is largely infused into all the composer's music. [. . .] This is unquestionably true, and it is the national element which gives to the music much of its freshness and charm.[15]

Unlike their US counterparts in the early 1880s, these British critics heard Dvořák's national "infusions" as assets rather than liabilities. But the landscape would change rapidly in the United States through the efforts of *New York Tribune* critic Henry Krehbiel, one of Corder's kindred spirits.[16]

KREHBIEL'S SOLUTION

Henry Edward Krehbiel, a second-generation German American from Ann Arbor, Michigan, spent most of his youth in the heavily German-speaking Cincinnati before moving to New York in 1880 (see figure 4.1). This environment imbued Krehbiel with a profound

FIGURE 4.1. Henry Krehbiel (1854–1923). Courtesy Music Division, New York Public Library for the Performing Arts.

appreciation of German music. Reflecting on the robust activity of Cincinnati's German choral societies, he remarked that "now the influence of Cincinnati Festivals goes out like leaven through the whole lump of American musical activity. [. . .] Chicago, Philadelphia, Buffalo, and Cleveland all strive to follow in the footsteps of Cincinnati, whose patriotic singers, encouraged by a patriotic public, go on adding triumph after triumph." Catholic in his musical tastes, he praised the 1884 Cincinnati May Festival for programming Beethoven's Ninth, "the fountain of inspiration at which Wagner, and Berlioz and Liszt, have drunk deep draughts," as well as Brahms's German Requiem, "the best example in all literature of music of the style pursued by the school in Germany that is striving to work out the musical progress in other lines than those adopted by Wagner's disciples."[17]

Like many German speakers of his generation, he defined German national identity through its cosmopolitanism. And the most complete musical expression of this identity was the symphony. In one of his earliest reviews for the *Tribune*, he expounded at length on the increasing presence and popularity of non-Germans on orchestral programs:

> We are threatened with a flood of "skis" and "ceks" and "viches." [...] Scandinavian [musical] sources having been industriously worked until their charm has failed, expectation now turns its face toward St. Petersburg, Prague, and Moscow, and if the present tendency is not checked, the people who have mastered the pronunciation of Winiauski [*sic*] and Tschaikowski, will have to extend their efforts to Moskowski, Arenski, Siloti, Mihalovich, Dvořák, Reznicek, Oudricek, and a dozen other names equally distorted as regards spelling. It is a useful fermentation which the introduction of this element has started in German music. As yet the composers mentioned do not seem to have created a type of art for themselves, but have contented themselves with infusing established forms with characteristic color and some of the fresh energy which can always be drawn from the reservoir of National folk-tunes.[18]

Showing clear national allegiance, he had complained two weeks earlier that the "charms" of Frederic Cowen's "Scandinavian" Third Symphony had "begun to decay though they are not more than two years before the world. They have not yet the vitality that marks the work of the foremost symphonists even when the scope of his composition is modest." It had not transcended what Krehbiel thought was a clunky welding of "national" and "universal" (German) styles.[19]

Critics on both sides of the aesthetic spectrum followed Krehbiel's lead by applauding symphonies that infused local color into a solidly "German" core. While praising the folksy melodies of Cowen's "Welsh" Fourth Symphony, Albert Steinberg of the *New York Herald* noted approvingly that even though it had an evocative national subtitle, "it is unmarked either by the cloying harmony or eccentricities of the modern German school" and "is not marred by the tricks and petty expedients which is apt to degenerate into noise." The Wagnerian Henry Finck, on the other hand, found the same piece lacking: "Mr. Cowen's work does not contain sufficient Welsh 'local color' to be quaintly interesting on that account, and the musical merit is small if viewed from the side of invention, while the scoring is, of course, excellent from the technical point of view." In other words, a conservative critic was likely to favor a "national" symphony so long as it wasn't *too* national, whereas a progressive was likely to criticize it for not being national *enough*. (Krehbiel, incidentally, was also unimpressed.)[20]

Echoing Frederick Corder, Krehbiel eventually settled on a solution to a fruitful musical future: a deeper infusion of folk music into German models. With a small nod to the ongoing aesthetic dispute, he elaborated on this philosophy at length in the introduction to a pamphlet recounting the highlights of the 1885–86 New York concert season:

> Since the rise of instrumental music all of the European "schools," without exception, have been the fruit of imitation. [. . .] In each of these cases there was an element of national character which was imitated from the Folksong of the respective people, but the force that impressed this element upon the artistic music of the world, which introduced the characteristic flavor into the art works written in the classic forms, or which made them modify those forms in order that the vessel might better hold the contents, was the individual genius of the men who struck out the new paths.[21]

And he made his ultimate purpose for presenting these ideas abundantly clear: "There is no reason why the same kind of thing should not take place in this country."

DVOŘÁK OF THE FUTURE

The multifaceted patterns of reception that had followed Dvořák into the mid-1880s persisted in the months leading up to his 1892 arrival in the United States. In the early 1890s, for example, a critic for the *Musical Standard* of London and Henry Finck of the *New York Evening Post* described the Eighth Symphony approvingly as "cosmopolitan" but reached the conclusion while looking through opposite aesthetic lenses:

> MUSICAL STANDARD: [The symphony] lacked any example of Sclavonicism. The four movements not only conform to

classic models, but they show Dvořák as a **cosmopolitan** rather than as a national musician.[22]

EVENING POST: There is less of the national element in it than in some of his earlier works, and the Bohemian is evidently becoming more and more **cosmopolitan**. [. . .] In the second part of the adagio there is a suggestion of the Titurel music from *Parsifal*.[23]

In a review of the symphonic variations, meanwhile, a critic for the *Brooklyn Daily Eagle* took this praise one step farther by arguing that Dvořák was a consummate artist capable of crossing all possible divides:

There is good, healthy paganism in them. A not very interesting theme is chosen as the text, and this is turned and altered and paraphrased in a surprising variety of ways, with many novel effects in orchestration and other effects as coarse and noisy as those of a street band. The music is now as wild as that of a gypsy dance, anon it is as suave as the love songs of Gounod; now it takes the measure of a jig and stopping in the middle of it describes, with solemnity, a cathedral service; yet in all the variations, fantastic and barbaric as they sometimes are, the hearer detects an undercurrent of depth and power that ever and again wells upward through the sounding surface of the theme.[24]

With this level of compositional dexterity allegedly at Dvořák disposal, it's no wonder that Frederick Corder had argued that he would be *the* symphonist of the future.

Corder's essay recirculated widely in the US press in 1890, rejuvenating Dvořák's supporters and convincing a few doubters of his superiority. None other than Krehbiel himself validated Corder's prediction of Dvořák's compositional ascendancy in a sweeping biographical essay appearing less than a month before the Bohemian's arrival in the United States:

> The significance of his compositions lies in their blending together of popular elements in classical forms. These forms were as romantic, as free, in their origin as the people's songs and dances; and in the hands of genius they will always remain pliant and plastic, in spite of the operations of that too zealous conservatism that masquerades as classicism.
>
> There is measureless comfort in the prospect which the example of Dvořák has opened up. It promises freshness and forcefulness of melodic, harmonic, and rhythmic contents, and newness and variety in the vehicles of utterance. It drives away the bugaboo of formlessness, which for so long a time has frightened the souls of fearful conservatives, by pointing the way to a multifarious development of forms.[25]

Indeed, even Arthur Mees, annotator of the New York Philharmonic's programs who called Dvořák "an apostle of absolute music" would come around to Krehbiel's point of view when he described the folk-inspired New World Symphony as a piece so "spontaneous and vigorous in conception and masterly in every detail of construction [that] it cannot but appeal to everyone musically receptive, of whatever nationality he may be." And in the context of Jim Crow America, the transcendence of nationality was a profoundly unmistakable metaphor for the assimilation of "ethnic" European immigrants into white racial dominance.[26]

NOTES

1. "The First Philharmonic Rehearsal," *NYT*, 7 Nov. 1894; "The First Philharmonic Concert," *NYTr*, 18 Nov. 1894; "Debut of Eugène Ysaÿe," *AAJ*, 24 Nov. 1894, 117.
2. Jürgen Osterhammel, *The Transformation of the World: A Global History of the Nineteenth Century*, trans. Patrick Camiller (Princeton, NJ: Princeton University Press), 403–7 and 826–37.
3. Matthew Gelbart, *The Invention of "Folk Music" and "Art Music": Emerging Categories from Ossian to Wagner* (New York: Cambridge University Press, 2007), 102–10; La Roche, "National Music," *American Quarterly Review*, June 1835, 279–80.
4. Gelbart, *The Invention*, 180–86.
5. Ibid., 191–204.
6. See Matthew D. Morrison, "Race, Blacksound, and the (Re)Making of Musicological Discourse," *Journal of the American Musicological Society* 72 (2019): 781–823.
7. Shadle, *Orchestrating the Nation*, 35–133.
8. Ibid., 158–72; Lavallée, "Dr. Louis Maas' Symphony, 'On the Prairies,'" *AAJ*, Jan. 20, 1882, 242–43.
9. Stevenson, "Music," *Indep*, 11 Jan. 1883, 9; "The Philharmonic Society," *NYTr*, 7 Jan. 1883; "Boston Symphony Orchestra," *BET*, 29 Oct. 1883; Proteus, "Boston Notes," *MV*, Dec. 1883, 324.
10. "Philharmonic Society," *AAJ*, 13 Jan. 1883, 225.
11. Brodbeck, *Defining Deutschtum*, 143–81.
12. Mark Evan Bonds, *Music as Thought: Listening to the Symphony in the Age of Beethoven* (Princeton, NJ: Princeton University Press, 2006) 63–103; Brodbeck, *Defining Deutschtum*, 181–82.
13. "Crystal Palace," *MT*, 1 May 1882, 263.
14. Corder, "The Future of the Symphony," *Quarterly Musical Review*, Feb. 1885, 41–42.
15. "Music: The Week," *Athenaeum*, 2 May 1885, 575.
16. J.B., "Philharmonic Society," *MW*, 25 Apr. 1885, 264.
17. Krehbiel, "The Festival," *MV*, May 1884, 117; Joseph Horowitz, *Moral Fire: Musical Portraits from America's Fin-de-Siécle* (Berkeley: University of California Press, 2012), 78–80.
18. "Brooklyn Philharmonic Society," *NYTr*, 2 Mar. 1884.
19. "New-York Philharmonic Society," *NYTr*, 17 Feb. 1884.
20. "New York Philharmonic," *NYH*, 11 Apr. 1885; "Last Philharmonic Concert," *NYEP*, 13 Apr. 1885; "A New Symphony," *NYTr*, 12 Apr. 1885.
21. H. E. Krehbiel, *Review of the New York Musical Season, 1885–1886* (New York and London: Novello, Ewer, and Co., 1886), xx–xxi.
22. "Philharmonic Society," *Musical Standard*, 3 May 1890, 409

23 "Recent Concerts," *NYEP*, 14 Mar. 1892.
24 "Philharmonic Concert," *BDE*, 22 Dec. 1888.
25 Krehbiel, "Antonín Dvořák," *Century Illustrated Magazine*, Sep. 1892, 657.
26 See Matthew Frye Jacobson, *Whiteness of a Different Color: European Immigrants and the Alchemy of Race* (Cambridge, MA: Harvard University Press, 1998).

CHAPTER 5
THE BREWING STORM

March 19, 1892—Dresden, Germany

The air in the lobby of the Gewerbehaus was thick with curious excitement as throngs of local music lovers filed in to hear August Trenkler's orchestra present an all-American program. Some people caught a glimpse of the great pianist Anton Rubinstein and composer Jean Louis Nicodé. What did the stars of this young country have to offer?

The conductor, Franz Xavier Arens, strode confidently on stage, and the orchestra greeted him as if he were one of their own. Confused looks all around: Music that sounded like Schumann, Mendelssohn, and Wagner.

Antonín Dvořák's New World Symphony. Douglas W. Shadle, Oxford University Press (2021). © Oxford University Press. DOI: 10.1093/oso/9780190645625.003.0005

But the names were Gleason, Chadwick, and Paine. Minute after minute of this stale music lulled a few people to sleep.

Suddenly a triangle. A rattling tambourine. Pizzicato strings in strange harmonies. After a pause, the most raucous music anyone had ever heard! A sinewy melody in the violins. Bouncing rhythms. What in the American South could elicit such sounds? After a shriek in the violins, a somber funeral march. Slow, labored, movement. Before long, the rollicking begins again and rises to a chaotic climax—THUMP THUMP THUMP!

The crowd leapt to its feet, cheering and calling for more. Even Rubinstein could be seen pointing to the stage and yelling, "Now that I like!" Evidently *this* American composer, Henry Schoenefeld, had something new to say.

Throughout the nineteenth century, and even beyond, many Americans believed that a folk-inspired song repertoire equivalent to those in Scotland, Switzerland, Scandinavia, or Eastern Europe was on the horizon. The chief impediment to its formation, they argued, remained the country's ancestral heterogeneity, even among the privileged groups of Western Europeans who could claim English, German, French, or Dutch heritage. Some kind of cultural amalgamation, perhaps strengthened by collective resolve in the face of a crisis, would allow this national repertoire to arise spontaneously. At least that's what many people hoped would happen. But this idealized amalgamation process ignored the realities of segregation, disenfranchisement, brutalization, and relocation of nonwhite racial and ethnic groups, even those with legal US citizenship. Many white Americans resisted any hint of social mixture with these groups.

In the final quarter of the century, a small contingent of white American composers cut against the grain by arguing in favor of using "authentic" nonwhite folk music as the basis of a national classical style. But, mirroring the exploitative commercial music market, their appropriation of nonwhite musical material perpetuated longstanding racist stereotypes of "barbarism," "exoticism," or "orientalism," merely reinforcing prevailing attitudes of white European cultural superiority. These musicians rarely acknowledged that nonwhite composers might wish to take their own musical heritage in new creative directions or that they might wish to participate in these discussions in the first place.[1]

Meanwhile, critic Henry Krehbiel also encouraged composers not to wait for cultural amalgamation to begin writing "national" music, arguing that they might consider other local sources of inspiration. He wrote in 1886, for example, that to create a distinctively American "school" of composition,

> Only two conditions are necessary—a strong exemplar, and popular encouragement. Foreign musicians have recognized a marked originality in the character of musical thought

and mode of expression in many of the efforts which have been timidly put forth by American writers, and simple melodies which have come from the untutored musicians of our minstrel halls have exerted a charm the world over. Unquestionably, with the development of the national type of character, which must wait for an amalgamation of the many heterogeneous elements of our present population, will come also a national feeling and manner of expression which will tincture our music in the same degree as our literature. Our political institutions, our rugged mountains, broad prairies, vast forests, magnificent lakes and rivers, will care for that. But we do not need to wait for the amalgam to become fixed before founding the "school."[2]

From his perspective, certain (unnamed) American composers had already moved in the appropriate direction. By the time Dvořák was well on his way to New York, Krehbiel had become convinced that the Bohemian guest would provide both necessary conditions for their continued success. "In Dvořák and his works," he wrote in the days before Dvořák arrived, "is to be found a twofold encouragement for the group of native musicians whose accomplishments of late have seemed to herald the rise of a school of American composers."[3]

Others remained doubtful. As news of Dvořák's impending appointment to the conservatory was spreading in 1891, a critic for the *Chicago Tribune* warned:

> Those who are familiar with his school of composition will fail to see in what way it can expedite American music. Pan Dvořák is preëminently a Slavic composer. All his music has the Slavic rhythm, color, and feeling. In one instance, his oratorio,

he sought to depart from it and to produce a composition on German and English lines, only to make a conspicuous failure. That he can found an American school or influence American music sufficiently to individualize it and give it a permanent standing admits of grave doubt.[4]

Even Dvořák himself was skeptical. In an exclusive interview for the *Chicago Tribune* published a month later, the reporter raised the question of American national opera—Thurber's pet project. After explaining that a libretto on a uniquely American subject was a distinct possibility, Dvořák turned his attention to music: "O, that is another thing. America can have native music, but national music never. There is no nationality in music. The libretto may be American and performers American, but no such thing as American music any more than German or French music. Americans will have to reflect the influence of the great German composers just as all countries do." So much for an American school![5]

But Dvořák would change his tune, quite literally, a few months into his residency. In an interview printed only a week after his potent statement about using "negro melodies" as the foundation of an American style, he clarified that "there is such a thing as nationality in music in the sense that it may take on the character of its locality"—a complete about-face influenced heavily by his personal engagement with baritone Harry T. Burleigh. Krehbiel's second condition for a national school had thus been met: popular encouragement. And with the final ink drying on Dvořák's new symphony, the world could hear the results.[6]

"NEGRO MELODIES" AS SOURCE

Well into the twenty-first century, it is still widely believed that Dvořák introduced Americans to the idea of using "negro melodies" as a source of compositional inspiration. But Krehbiel clearly thought that a folk-based school of composition was already taking shape and could benefit from Dvořák's cultivation. At the time, musicians considered pianist Louis Moreau Gottschalk the first US-born composer to infuse the "spirit" of African-derived folksongs into instrumental music. While studying in France as a teenager, he wrote pieces for solo piano based on Afro-Caribbean melodies he had learned as a child in the multiracial environment of New Orleans. These works secured him an international reputation as a distinctively American composer during his lifetime, and this legacy followed him after his sudden death in 1869 at the age of forty.

Gottschalk's friend, editor and critic Henry Cood Watson, used his music magazine, the *American Art Journal,* as a vehicle for preserving this national legacy, once arguing that Gottschalk's "genius is the one great musical luster, which Americans can claim as belonging exclusively to themselves, or to the nation." After Watson's own death in 1875, his protégé William Thoms took up the mantle: "We are not half as proud of the memory of this truly great American composer as we should be. [. . .] The scientific knowledge [he] obtained was used in a full measure to poetically clothe the rude forms of the characteristic melodies of his native soil." Thoms's invocation of "native" folk infusions anticipated Dvořák's formula by fifteen years.[7]

The 1881 publication of Gottschalk's memoir, *Notes of a Pianist*, sparked renewed interest in his career that gathered more widespread momentum for the development of a folk-based American style. Amy Fay, a former student of Franz Liszt and one of the country's foremost pianists, read the memoir in 1884 and reported her impressions in the *American Art Journal*:

> In spite of his foreign education, his compositions are the product of the sunny South, in which he was born. Many of them even drew their inspiration from the negro melodies which he heard as a child. [. . .] In these compositions he has preserved the poetry and melancholy of that picturesque race, and they have, therefore, a national value.[8]

In a lecture given at the annual convention of the Music Teachers National Association later that summer, Boston composer George E. Whiting also anticipated Dvořák by pointing to Gottschalk as the model of a future national style:

> There is, however, one field of local color in this country, and which has been but little used, which I would like to call to the attention of composers. I refer to the melodies of the Creoles of the South and Cuba. Gottschalk is really the only American who has ever succeeded in producing compositions founded on subjects from his own land.[9]

Heralding a dramatic shift in the compositional landscape, Whiting added, "I fully believe that his compositions will be much better known in the future than they are now."

Another composer of Gottschalk's generation, Ellsworth Phelps of Brooklyn, took a similar stylistic approach in his

1880 "Emancipation Symphony." A six-movement titan, the symphony attempted to depict enslaved people on plantations, the Civil War, and Abraham Lincoln's funeral procession before climaxing in a choral setting of abolitionist poet John Greenleaf Whittier's triumphal "Laus Deo." An advance description explained that "the profound pathos of all the negro melodies, which haunts one with a sense of suffering long drawn and almost hopeless, characterizes the first and second movements, the latter giving way to an exquisite tone picture of the lights and shades of Southern slave life."[10]

As Phelps was completing the "Emancipation Symphony," a New Orleans novelist named George Washington Cable had begun collecting examples of Creole folksongs with the intent of publishing them in the *Century Magazine*, a literary monthly. One of Henry Krehbiel's childhood friends, Lafcadio Hearn, began helping Cable in 1878 and sent Krehbiel many of their findings. In turn, Krehbiel enlisted the help of another Cincinnati friend, composer John Broekhoven (see figure 5.1), to create a three-movement instrumental suite based on the melodies Hearn sent him. This new piece, called *Suite Creole*, premiered at a private soirée hosted by the city's elite in 1884. Krehbiel traveled from New York so that he could give a speech explaining the music.[11]

Broekhoven's suite took on a life of its own after he created a version for full orchestra that premiered at a Cincinnati resort in July 1884. Previewing the concert, a writer for the *Enquirer* remarked,

FIGURE 5.1. Drawing of John Broekhoven, *Musical Courier*, 9 Dec. 1885. Courtesy RIPM Retrospective Index to Music Periodicals, www.ripm.org.

The ideas therein presented were gathered from quaint examples of the creole or negro melodies that are just now attracting wide-spread attention. Unadorned, their intrinsic value is slight, but the composer has elaborated and filled them out with such a wealth of imaginative genius evidenced in the work that they fairly glisten with bright thoughts.[12]

After a performance in Nashville the following May, the suite aroused national attention at the Boston MTNA convention in 1886. By 1889, critic John S. Van Cleve felt comfortable enough putting Broekhoven on a level with his European counterparts in a review of Heinrich Hoffmann's *Bilder aus Norden*: "Liszt, Brahms, and Dvořák have used the melodies of the Huns and Bohemians. Bizet has given us his *Suite Arlesienne*. The music of Scandinavia has been used by Grieg and others, while the grotesque pathos of our American Africans furnished our local musician, Broekhoven, with the subject matter of his *Suite Creole*." The suite made its New York debut in 1891 at a concert hosted by the Manuscript Society, and a committee chose it to be one of eight pieces by US composers performed at the 1893 Chicago World's Fair. By that point, it was quite possibly the only American orchestral piece with such a wide audience.[13]

Composer Henry Schoenefeld of Chicago followed in Broekhoven's footsteps by writing a suite for strings with a second movement, marked "Marcio-Fantastico," that supposedly depicted "Southern negro life." Unlike Broekhoven, Schoenefeld did not draw directly from known folksongs but added tambourine, triangle, and tam-tam to expand the work's color palette with stereotyped "African" exoticism reminiscent of blackface minstrelsy. Conductor Theodore Thomas first programmed the suite at the 1890 MTNA convention in Detroit, and it received performances in Milwaukee and Chicago under Schoenefeld's own direction over the next year. The Milwaukee audience demanded an encore of the second movement.[14]

FIGURE 5.2. Frank Saddler, *Klänge aus Amerika* (1891), Bayerischen Staatsbibliothek München, 2 Mus.pr. 4058, p. 5, urn:nbn:de:bvb:12-bsb00051977-2. Courtesy Bayerischen Staatsbibliothek München.

By the time Dvořák arrived in September 1892, several white composers were already experimenting with various ways to construct a characteristically American style based on African-derived folk music. But their use of the material ranged from outright quotation of transcribed sources (Broekhoven) to reimagined settings of Negro spirituals (Phelps) to the sonic stereotypes of the blackface minstrel stage (Schoenefeld). None of these composers had acquired their material in direct collaboration with Black musicians, as Dvořák eventually would. Their impulse to appropriate material for their own professional gain mirrored the practice of French musicians like Claude Debussy, who borrowed from the "exotic" Asian music he encountered at the 1889 Paris World's Fair—a quintessential encapsulation of the European imperial "civilizing mission."[15]

SPARKS FROM THE EAST

In the final weeks of 1891, Jeannette Thurber announced that the National Conservatory would give a boost to American composers by offering large cash prizes for the best opera, libretto, symphony, oratorio, suite or cantata, and concerto. According to advertisements, Dvořák would head the selection committee after his arrival. But in the months leading up to Dvořák's residency, an endorsement of the emerging American national style came from Europe, where audiences responded enthusiastically to pieces in this vein.[16]

Frank E. Saddler, a young Pittsburgh composer studying in Munich, had impressed German crowds in May 1891 with his orchestral potpourri, *Klänge aus Amerika*, or *Sounds from America* (see figure 5.2). Rather than an original composition, it was a dramatically scored "potpourri" of eighteen "national melodies," including patriotic songs ("Yankee Doodle"), Stephen Foster songs ("Old Folks at Home"), and minstrel songs ("Dixie"). The *Pittsburgh Dispatch* reported that the Munich premiere "won repeated recalls" and was given "a liberal offer for its publication." The cover of the published piano reduction nevertheless exploited regional and racial stereotypes in order to appeal to European consumers unaware of the complex post-Reconstruction social landscape in the United States.[17]

And certain European musicians found much to enjoy. Critic Charles Scoville of the *Dispatch* reported, for example, that famed Bayreuth conductor Hermann Levi believed that the songs Saddler had chosen might serve as the foundation of a truly national style, describing them as "no less characteristic and much fresher than the Hungarian national airs, of which Brahms has made such notable use." As news about Levi's opinion circulated in the national press, at least one commentator raised concerns that Saddler was representing the country with "cheap tunes." But a writer for the *Musical Courier* retorted that Gottschalk had "found a wealth of original melodies south of the Mason and Dixon line" and that Broekhoven had "taken creole themes for his well-known suite." If Europeans enjoyed the music, Scoville asked, "is this not something creditable for our musical reputation?"[18]

Another musical missionary, conductor Franz Xavier Arens, led concerts featuring only American composers throughout Europe in the summers of 1891 and 1892 (see figure 5.3). During his second tour, which included stops in Berlin, Dresden, Leipzig, Weimar, and Vienna, the unusual

FIGURE 5.3. Drawing of Franz Xavier Arens, *Musical Courier*, 10 Aug. 1892. Courtesy RIPM Retrospective Index to Music Periodicals, www.ripm.org.

second movement of Henry Schoenefeld's suite proved to be a hit. A Dresden correspondent to the *Musical Courier* wrote that the "lively and characteristic negro melodies are of great freshness and peculiarity and were greeted with acclamation, which always will be the case with every composition or national tune of some special coloring."

A critic at the Vienna concert called the movement the "most specifically American" piece on the program, while another, enchanted by its "whimsically grotesque structure," remarked that the rest of Arens's program "smells of European models"—the "triumvirate of Schumann, Wagner, and Liszt."[19]

As the good news about Schoenefeld's suite rolled in from abroad, several skeptics came out of the woodwork. George H. Wilson, an editor of Boston's *Musical Herald*, accused Arens of harming the prospects of American composers by creating segregated programs. "The [national] label," he wrote, "should be torn from the wrapper and Mr. Reinecke of Leipsic, Mr. Fischer of Munich, Mr. Richter of Vienna, and the others be asked to judge the contents simply as music." Although he didn't mention Schoenefeld specifically, the mixed European reception of Arens's patriotic programs concerned him. Krehbiel agreed, arguing that "there was no prejudice against our composers to be overcome in Europe, and, to be entirely frank in the matter, there was nothing novel, characteristic, or particularly striking in what our composers had to say to their colleagues abroad." He appended two negative Viennese reviews to prove the point. In short, Wilson and Krehbiel felt that if American compositions couldn't hold their own against European compositions on the same program, they shouldn't be heard at all.[20]

William Thoms of the *American Art Journal*, a noted champion of US composers, hoped to draw attention away from the scuffle by publishing an essay on Gottschalk written by Chicago music theorist A. J. Goodrich. "It was his destiny," Goodrich wrote, "to imbibe and to express in his compositions the plaints and revels, the tears and laughter of that strange, antipodean condition—American slave life." After analyzing the motivic construction of Gottschalk's *Bamboula*, Goodrich went on to explain why keeping the pianist's compositional techniques in mind was so important with Dvořák's impending arrival:

> During the past season Mr. Arens gave orchestral concerts in Berlin and Dresden, the programs of which were composed exclusively of American works. Curiosity was sufficiently piqued to ensure Mr. Arens good sized audiences; but the critics were very sparing of their praise until Henry Schoenefeld's characteristic Suite was performed. Ah, they said, here is something new,—something not familiar to European ears! What was it? Nothing more or less than an American plantation melody worked out in various movements. The quaint rhythm, the plaintive grotesqueness of the tune attracted instant attention, for here was a motive not already developed by Brahms, Dvořák, Saint-Saëns, Grieg or Tschaikowski. [. . .] Mr. Schoenefeld was therefore wise in following the example of Gottschalk, and if our American composers at the present time wish to produce works distinctly American they must resuscitate the old slave melodies, or the Indian ghost dances, and make these the motives of their symphonies, suites, and concertos.[21]

Readers learned a few weeks later that Anton Rubinstein, the great pianist now living in Dresden, had "clapped his hands after the performance of Schoenefeld's suite and loudly ejaculated: 'Now, that I like!' " If European luminaries enjoyed the supposedly American national style crafted by Schoenefeld and others, its future in the United States seemed secure.[22]

NOTES

1. See Lynn Abbot and Doug Seroff, *Out of Sight: The Rise of African American Popular Music, 1889–1895* (Jackson: University Press of Mississippi, 2002).
2. Krehbiel, *Review*, xxi.
3. Krehbiel, "Antonín Dvořák," 657.
4. "New York Gets Dvořák," *ChiTr*, 13 Sep. 1891.
5. "How Dvořák Conducts," *ChiTr*, 4 Oct. 1891.
6. "Real Value of Negro Melodies," *NYH*, 21 May 1893; "Antonín Dvořák on Negro Melodies," *NYH*, 28 May 1893.
7. "Gottschalk's Posthumous Works," *WAJ*, 7 Mar. 1874, 228; "Louis Moreau Gottschalk," *AAJ*, 4 May 1878, 4.
8. Fay, "Louis Moreau Gottschalk," *AAJ*, 12 July 1884, 177.
9. Whiting, "An American School of Composition," *AAJ*, 30 Aug. 1884, 291.
10. "A Brooklyn Composer," *BDE*, 16 Nov. 1879; Shadle, *Orchestrating the Nation*, 205–10.
11. Elizabeth Bisland, *The Life and Letters of Lafcadio Hearn* (Boston and New York: Houghton Mifflin, 1906), 1:175–76; "Soloists Entertained," *CinCG*, 22 May 1884.
12. "Musical," *CinEn*, 13 Jul. 1884.
13. "Nashville Honors Herself," *Nashville Daily American*, 22 May 1885; "Friday's Meeting," *MC*, 7 July 1886, 5; "Sunday Afternoon Concert at Music Hall," *CinCG*, 24 Feb. 1889; "The American Compositions," *AAJ*, 25 Apr. 1891, 20; "Music at the Fair," *ChiTr*, 5 Aug. 1893.
14. "MTNA," *MC*, 2 July 1890, 4; "Amusements," *Milwaukee Sentinel*, 18 Feb. 1891; "It Was Thomas Night," *ChiTr*, 8 Nov. 1891.
15. See Annegret Fauer, *Musical Encounters at the 1889 Paris World's Fair* (Rochester, NY: University of Rochester Press, 2005), 195–206.
16. "Music and Patriotism," *WaPo*, 22 Nov. 1891.
17. "The Success of a Pittsburgher," *PD*, 24 May 1891.
18. "America's National Airs," *PD*, 12 July 1891; "Mr. Charles Scoville," *MC*, 22 July 1891, 82.
19. "Dresden Letter," *MC*, 13 Apr. 1892, 8; "Von der Internationalen Musik- und Theater-Ausstellung," *Musikalisches Wochenblatt*, 29 Sep. 1892, 490; "Ausstellungskonzerte," *Allgemeine Kunst-Chronik*, 10 July 1892, 15 (my translations).
20. Wilson, "A Chronicle," *BMH*, July 1892, 147–48; "American Music in Vienna," *NYTr*, 24 July 1892.
21. Goodrich, "Gottschalk as Composer and Pianist," *AAJ*, 2 July 1892, 295.
22. "Flickers," *AAJ*, 16 July 1892, 353.

CHAPTER 6
THE FIERY DEBATE

January 23, 1894—New York City

Some of the city's most distinguished residents gathered at the Madison Square Garden Concert Hall for the National Conservatory's student charity concert in support of the *Herald*'s clothing fund drive. The program's main attraction was Black soprano Sissieretta Jones, and everyone paid top dollar for the honor of attending. It was for a good cause, after all.

As Dr. Dvořák settled on the podium, he waved his baton to launch Mendelssohn's overture to *A Midsummer Night's Dream*. The student orchestra had spirit but was too ragged for its charms. After their nerves had calmed, they sounded far better in Robert Volkmann's second serenade for strings, especially as they breathed sweet air into the dashing waltz.

One of Adele Margulies's piano students, a child, walked onto the stage and gave Dr. Dvořák a deep bow, telling him, "I am quite ready." And ready she was: Her fiery rendition of Liszt's *Hungarian Fantasy* prompted the director to waive school policy and grant her an encore.

Whistles and cheers greeted Jones as she walked on stage to sing Rossini's penetrating "Inflammatus" accompanied by a choir of more than one hundred Black students from the conservatory. Her high notes were effortless, and she responded to shouts for an encore with a stunning aria from Meyerbeer's *Robert le Diable*.

One of Dvořák's composition students, Maurice Arnold, then took the podium to lead a series of "Plantation Dances," his own effort to create a uniquely American style.

As soon as Dvořák retook the stage along with Jones and baritone Harry T. Burleigh, a student so successful he was raised to faculty status, a young violinist jumped up to hand the maestro an ebony baton with a gold handle—a sign of appreciation. There wasn't a dry eye in the house.

"Seeing that Dr. Dvořák is the apostle of national music," a reviewer for the *Herald* remarked the next day, "the first number he directed with his baton was his own arrangement of America's most popular folk song, 'The Old Folks at Home.'" The concert netted over $1,000 (see figure 6.1).[1]

HEAR THE "OLD FOLKS AT HOME."

It Will Be Rendered To-Night for Charity as It Has Never Been Before.

DVORAK'S OWN ARRANGEMENT.

It Will Be Sung Entirely by Negroes, of Whom Mme. Jones, the "Black Patti," Is Soloist.

AID FOR THE CLOTHING FUND.

Donations Are Still Coming in, but There Is Still a Great Need of Women's Wear.

FIGURE 6.1. Headline for "Old Folks at Home." *New York Herald*, 23 Jan. 1894.

In the months leading up to Dvořák's arrival, critics at home and abroad compelled white American composers to work through a stylistic calculus that might have looked like this:

1. How closely should I follow conventional formal models? Go too far in either direction and I'll be accused of backwardness or decadence. Either way, I run the risk of being labeled a European imitator.
2. How can I give my music a distinct national identity? The United States doesn't have a robust folk music tradition, but some possibilities are available.
3. If I attempt to infuse my music with folk elements, where should they come from? Popular songs? Patriotic songs? Louis Moreau Gottschalk was successful with Creole songs in the past, and critics are finding new value in his approach.

Composers John Broekhoven, Frank Saddler, and Henry Schoenefeld had skirted the first question by choosing genres with few formal expectations—the suite and the potpourri. Following Gottschalk's lead, they had also sought inspiration in the folksongs of Black Americans and ultimately found enthusiastic audiences in cities around the United States and Germany. These overwhelmingly white groups were unlikely to question the propriety of white composers appropriating Black musical material or taking it upon themselves to depict African American life.

As successful as this style was in certain contexts, though, supporting it was still a minority position in 1892. In public discourse, nuanced questions about compositional technique were secondary to more fundamental concerns about the place of American composers within the musical economy—how their music reached the public or how they earned money. In the case of orchestral music, composers depended entirely on the generosity of conductors. The greatest orchestral piece in the world would make no difference if no one ever heard it. Ruminating about style was a luxury when the marketplace included a steady stream of new works from Europe *and* staples of the established repertoire.

Critics in the United States had ignored these fundamental realities for decades. Bostonian John Sullivan Dwight had once argued, "If a work has genius in it, it will sooner or later make its mark upon the world." For him, style didn't matter. "If a new Beethoven was born in America this very morning," he asked, "is not the world as sure to hear from him, and own him, as if he had sprung up under the guardianship of Liszt at Weimer, or of Hauptmann, Moscheles, and Co., at Leipsic? Time will take care of all these questions." George Wilson of the Boston *Musical Herald* would say essentially the same thing nearly forty years later: "American music should take its chances along with French and Russian or any other music, and bide its time."[2]

Although it avoided practical considerations like how to get on a program in the first place, this attitude reflected a pervasive belief in music's expressive universality—the idea that music can speak to all people equally since it expresses shared human feelings. Universalism proved to be an attractive proposition for many composers, too, because they believed success in the concert hall demonstrated their ability to bend music's powers to their individual wills and channel it to communicate effectively with audiences.

In the months leading up to Dvořák's arrival in the United States in 1892, leading magazines published commentaries by prominent composers indicating that they had no interest in pursuing distinctively American projects:

> FREDERIC GRANT GLEASON: It may be said of an American school of composition, that, like the Kingdom of Heaven, it "cometh not with observation." It is not at all necessary that the American composer should consciously strive to write in a style which should be characterized as "American" in the sense of differing from the peculiarities to be found in the works of writers belonging to other nationalities.[3]

> WILLIAM WALLACE GILCHRIST: Let us then, as Americans, strive not to follow this school or that, not for any fixed, deliberate, premeditated character in our work. [. . .] Let not future generations say: This is good because American, German, Italian, French. Let them say: This is good because true; beautiful because it is true.[4]

> EDWARD MACDOWELL: As for the remark in *The Musical Courier* that "Bach, Beethoven, Schumann, Mendelssohn, Liszt, Berlioz, and Wagner are some of the causes of the American composer," it is certainly true, but it is just as certainly true of every composer in the world (of no matter what nationality) who came after them. I for one am proud of the pedigree.[5]

Statements like these raised the stakes of Dvořák's residency. If he wanted to develop an American "national school," would the universalist majority consider him a meddler? And yet he couldn't possibly solve the equally universal problem of how to increase American representation on orchestral programs. It was all but inevitable that he would weigh in on these burning topics after he arrived. The only question was when.

"THE REAL VALUE OF NEGRO MELODIES"

Dvořák *did* weigh in just a few months after his arrival, and he came out in support of a style rooted in Black vernacular music. But how did he become so immersed in this music that he decided to pursue it himself and openly recommend it to others? His immediate musical circle included plausible sources who probably all worked on him in one way or another:

> THOMAS W. HIGGINSON: White Union colonel who had collected several texts of Negro spirituals while serving in the Civil War and published his findings in 1867.[6]
>
> JAMES HUNEKER: White critic who claimed to have shared both Broekhoven's *Suite Creole* and a magazine article from December 1892 that discusses the musical characteristics of Negro spirituals in exacting detail.[7]
>
> MAURICE ARNOLD: Composer of German ancestry (probably white) who reportedly inspired Dvořák to pursue the idea of "negro melodies" while a student in his composition class.[8]
>
> HARRY T. BURLEIGH: Black vocal student at the conservatory who recounted that Dvořák knew the repertoire of Negro spirituals because Burleigh "used to play and sing these songs for him" in the director's residence.[9]

HENRY KREHBIEL: White critic who had a strong research background with Creole songs and had been involved with the creation of John Broekhoven's suite.

HENRY SCHOENEFELD: White composer whom Dvořák called "my friend" in a letter to Theodore Thomas from April 1893; Dvořák had also seen the score to his *Rural Symphony* as part of the Conservatory's composition contest earlier that year.[10]

Although the degree of influence from each source is unclear, the article James Huneker showed Dvořák also speculated that "when our American musical Messiah sees fit to be born, he will then find ready to his hand a mass of lyrical and dramatic themes [i.e., Black vernacular music] with which to construct a distinctively American music." This idea would have appealed to Dvořák, who had come to see his role as a catalyst for this project. "The Americans expect great things from me," he had written to a friend not long after arriving. Now he had concrete ideas coming at him from several directions at once.[11]

When the *Herald* published Dvořák's famous interview under the headline "Real Value of Negro Melodies" in May 1893, his thoughts on the matter had become a "settled conviction." These are the interview's essential elements:

THESIS: "I am now satisfied that the future music of this country must be founded upon what are called negro melodies. This must be the real foundation of any serious and original school of composition to be developed in the United States."

RATIONALE: "All of the great musicians have borrowed from the songs of the common people. [. . .] Only in this way can a musician express the true sentiment of his people."

MUSICAL POTENTIAL: "They are pathetic, tender, passionate, melancholy, solemn, religious, bold, merry, gay or what you will. It is music that suits itself to any mood or any purpose. There is nothing in the whole age of composition that cannot be supplied with themes from this source."

COUNTEREXAMPLE: "It is a great pity that English musicians have not profited out of this rich store. Somehow the old Irish and Scotch ballads have not seized upon or appealed to them."

HOPE FOR THE FUTURE: "There is one young man upon whom I am building strong expectations [Arnold]. His compositions are based upon negro melodies, and I have encouraged him in this direction."

STIFF CHALLENGES: "The other members of the composition class seem to think that it is not in good taste to get ideas from the old plantation songs, but they are wrong."[12]

On the surface, these statements were no more likely to spark an international debate than anything respected Americans had expressed before international audiences in the past. But the interview's frame, written by journalist James Creelman, included politically potent material that set off alarm bells.[13]

The *Herald* had practically invented global journalistic sensationalism, and Creelman hit on multiple fronts. He opened the interview by calling Dvořák the "acknowledged leader" of the Wagnerian side in the aesthetic conflict—a blatant exaggeration bound to raise hackles in the musical world. But he also equated Dvořák's positions on Black music with genuine sympathy for people of African descent—a far more explosive insinuation in an article designed to be read around the country. White mobs lynched Black Americans at a pace of three to four incidents per week in 1893, while state legislatures had already enshrined racial segregation and nonwhite disenfranchisement with Jim Crow laws. Creelman and the *Herald* had set up Dvořák for vicious responses.

THE FIRESTORM

In a tightly orchestrated effort, the *Herald* story made an immediate global impact after going to print in late May. The newspaper's European edition, based in Paris, ran followup stories throughout the week, while the New York edition ran fresh coverage and portions of the European material in a controlled burn over the next two. Regular concert seasons were over, so music news was otherwise relatively light. This strategy allowed enough time for news wires around the country to pick up pieces of the story, especially through digestible briefs designed for smaller newspapers that couldn't devote resources to original coverage. By June 6, dozens of outlets from coast to coast had given space to the story, leading the *Herald* editors to congratulate themselves on a job well done. "In presenting Dr. Dvořák's views on the future of American music," they crowed, "the *Herald* has precipitated worldwide discussion." As music magazines with international readerships weighed in with their slower release schedules, the story remained in circulation throughout the United States and Britain until the New World Symphony premiered on December 16.[14]

Creelman managed to field responses from prominent musicians in Berlin, Vienna, and Paris within a matter of days. Violinist Joseph Joachim, pianists Anton

Rubinstein and Sally Liebling, and composer Ernest Reyer all thought Dvořák's ideas made sense because so many European composers had already succeeded with similar strategies. Composer Anton Bruckner, musicologist Eusebius Mandyczewski, and conductor Hans Richter—all of Vienna—threw what the *Herald* called a "cold-water douche" on the idea. Bruckner insisted that "the basis of all music must be found in the classical works of the past," while the others felt that educated composers could never assimilate music from an oral tradition (what they perceived Black vernacular music to be).[15]

The genuinely curious but disinterested comments from Europeans, which the *Herald* printed to raise the perceived stakes of the controversy, contrasted sharply with the dozens of impassioned responses, signed and unsigned, that would appear over the next several months in the US press. A debate about a seemingly esoteric subject relevant only to professional composers almost immediately careened out of control into a complex discussion mirroring broader intellectual debates about the very nature of American national identity—who was included and who got to decide.[16]

Whether Creelman's or Dvořák's, the choice to use the ambiguous phrase "negro melodies" launched a significant thread in the debate about what the phrase meant: the music of Southern enslaved people, Creole music of the gulf coast, African music, blackface minstrelsy, or some combination. Without rejecting Dvořák's ideas outright, early respondents from Boston used this ambiguity to question his credibility:

J. B. Claus: Mr. Dvořák must be excused for the mistake he makes, because he must naturally think the "Negro" is the original American instead of the imported slave, and if they sung any other melodies than those composed by white men, it must have been music from Africa.[17]

Napier Lothian: Mr. Dvořák is probably unaware of the sources whence are derived the songs sung by the minstrel companies, and he credits us [Americans] with more folksongs than we deserve.[18]

Others took a much firmer tone reflecting deep-seated anti-Black racism:

Philip Clayton Rogers: What melody has any darky ever evolved from his inner consciousness? As a matter of fact, all the celebrated negro melodies were composed, songs and music, by white men, notably at their head Steve Foster.[19]

Statements denying the creative ability of African American people appeared throughout the debate and were typically meant to paint Dvořák as a naïve foreigner. A writer for the notably sardonic *Freund's Weekly* in New York went so far as to insult Dvořák directly: "I learn on good authority that D. Antonín Dvořák, in order to give a 'couleure locale' to the symphony based on negro melodies, which he is now composing, blackens his face while closeted in his studio in search of nebulous inspiration. Why not? Satin gowns for Wagner; burnt cork for Dvořák."[20]

A few writers countered this perspective by invoking the widely held belief that people of African ancestry possessed "natural" musical talents. This "fact," they argued, was a good reason to be optimistic about Dvořák's ideas:

DAVID BRAHAM: The aptitude of the negro for music—one of the characteristic traits of the whole race—is really wonderful. Time and time again I have been impressed with the instinct of even the most ignorant of the negroes for music.[21]

ED HARRIGAN: The fact that the negro race possesses a remarkable facility for music is so familiar to everyone in this country that I am rather surprised no great authority in music has thought before this of taking the matter up.[22]

For others, this supposedly "natural" musicality was a defect that militated against the implementation of Dvořák's ideas:

> The negroes have a natural appreciation of melody and rhythm. [. . .] Water can never rise above its source. Savagery and gloom give but a feeble flame to light on to artistic greatness a race which, from the foundation of society, has been at the bottom of the scale. [. . .] How little, then, is to be hoped from the scant and savage strains of a servile race.[23]

In both cases, the stereotyped attribution of natural musicality to people of African ancestry was meant to illustrate a lack of intellectual capacity and therefore to distinguish them from white people, whose capacity to learn supposedly surpassed all others. Expanding on this pervasive racist stereotype, several other commentators expressed concerns that Black musicians might not be able to make an effective transition to a formal conservatory curriculum because of their ties to oral tradition, regardless of any "innate" talent.[24]

Discussions about the origins of "negro melodies" often overlapped with those about their suitability as a medium of American national expression. This second thread tended to attract input from well-known musicians who were already sympathetic to the idea of a distinctly American school. And most agreed that this repertoire was not a suitable source.

> AMY BEACH: Without the slightest desire to question the beauty of the negro melodies of which he speaks so highly, or to disparage them on account of their source, I cannot help feeling justified in the belief that they are not fully typical of our country.[25]
>
> REGINALD DE KOVEN: Are these negro melodies—interesting, characteristic, musically suggestive though they be—in any sense representative? That his is the dominant race-type whose soul utterances, as expressed in music, we will, so to speak, glorify by codification? This, one would think, the average American citizen would hardly wish to allow.[26]

Beach, De Koven, and others insisted that the country's diverse ethnic makeup meant that different groups had unique relationships to their own musical heritage that they could articulate in new compositions. Boston critic Louis Elson observed, for example, that "the United States is a world in itself, composed of many nations." But they failed to acknowledge that people of African ancestry ought to be considered full members of the American nation.[27]

Still another group rejected Dvořák's ideas altogether on the grounds that music is universal—that it can't express a national identity at all. Violinist and composer William Mollenhauer wrote a bitter letter to the *American Art Journal* that summed up practically every argument against Dvořák:

> These melodies are so incipient and trivial that an American would be ashamed to derive his inspiration from such trash; besides, the negro is a negro and belongs to Africa, not to America. These so-called negro songs are not original. [. . .] Have we Americans so little talent that we must derive our inspirations from such sources? Besides, art belongs to the world, not to one nation.[28]

Harvard professor John Knowles Paine made an even stronger appeal replete with white supremacist invective in an interview with the *Boston Herald*:

> It is not a question of nationality, but individuality, and individuality of style is not the result of limitation—whether of folk-songs, negro melodies, the tunes of the heathen Chinee or Digger Indians, but of personal character and inborn originality. During the present century musical art has overstepped all national limits; it is no longer a mere question of Italian, German, French, English, Slavonic or American music, but of world music.[29]

Paine went on to say that Dvořák must have been unaware of what American composers had already accomplished in genres like the symphony and that whoever transcribed the interview must have misunderstood what Dvořák had said. The editors of the *Musical Courier* in New York agreed. "Nationalism is a fatal rut for a composer to work in," they warned, for "the greatest composers, and those whose works are the most enduring, are not German, Hungarian, or French, they belong to the world."[30]

Amid the mudslinging and vitriol, however, Dvořák found an array of cautiously optimistic allies who thought American composers might as well give his ideas a chance.

George Osgood, a vocalist in Boston, used history as his guide:

> In making the statement that the development of a national school of American music depends upon the study of our negro melodies and their application to musical composition, Dvořák follows logically in the same path pursued by all his illustrious predecessors.[31]

Rubin Goldmark, Dvořák's own composition student and a nephew of Viennese composer Karl Goldmark, urged everyone to put details aside and focus on what mattered most:

> Here is something, then, distinctively American, that would, if properly treated, be recognized as such, irrespective of its origins or of the circumstances under which it flourished.[32]

He meant "negro melodies," of course. "With the resources that are at our command," he added, "may the American composer soon follow in the footsteps of his European contemporary."

But a final group reminded the public that Dvořák was not the first person to come up with this idea and debunked the notion that he should get any credit for it. Berlin-based composer Arthur Bird recalled Anton Rubinstein's reaction to Henry Schoenefeld's use of "negro melodies" in his suite, noting that "it seemed to interest [Rubinstein] very much." George Whiting told the *Boston Herald* that he agreed with Dvořák because "more than eight years ago in a paper read before the American Music Teachers' National Association I advocated the same thing." And an especially concerned musician wrote to the *New York Herald* to offer a historical correction:

> A. THOMPSON: This idea may be original with Dr. Dvořák, but George F. Bristow advanced that theory ten years ago and was laughed at for it. Bristow's idea was that the American school of music would partake more of the character of negro melody in the South than the so-called negro melodies sung at minstrel shows.[33]

The *Herald* created a special news brief about this seemingly inconsequential piece of trivia and circulated it widely throughout the country.[34]

THE DIRECTOR SPEAKS

Dvořák, meanwhile, had avoided the controversy through much of the summer. He was enjoying trips to places like Minnehaha Falls in Minnesota and the World's Columbian Exposition in Chicago, where he was an honored guest on Bohemian Day. While he was in Chicago, a reporter for the *Tribune* asked him to clarify his ideas about an American national style. Affirming his original statements, he explained:

> I do not mean to take these melodies, plantation, Creole or Southern, and work them out as themes; that is not my plan. But I study certain melodies until I become thoroughly imbued with their characteristics. The symphony is the least desirable of vehicles for the display of this work, in that the form will allow only a suggestion of the color of that nationalism to be given. Liberty in this line is never allowable.[35]

And his new symphony? "My new symphony," he continued, "is also on the same lines—namely: an endeavor to portray characteristics, such as are distinctively American. [. . .] Gottschalk also recognized and worked upon this plan." He probably felt that he would continue to find sympathy in certain corners of the musical world and that redoubling his statements would soften the lingering negativity.

The confusion should have died on the spot, but Dvořák's friend Anton Seidl, conductor of the New York Philharmonic, wrote a letter to the *New York Tribune* a month later outlining *his* thoughts about Dvořák's ideas, revealing his own anti-Black attitudes:

> It cannot be possible that he believes that a truly American, a new school of music, might be founded on negro melodies. As a help for composers who lack original ideas, certain black melodies (which moreover were for the greater part the inventions of white men) can be made useful in the construction of an overture, symphony, suite, or serenade. [. . .] A man of Dvořák's genius, whose strength lies in thematic workmanship, who builds up a colossal movement out of the most insignificant theme, would be able to make a black symphony out of black themes, although I fancy the multi-colored Dvořák would nevertheless be visible. There is the point—individuality will always remain the principal thing and will always assert itself, be the materials that it handles, colored or uncolored.[36]

After reprinting and commending this letter, the *Musical Courier* remarked that it had "been informed by one who has been permitted the honor of viewing the score of Dr. Dvořák's 'African' symphony that the work is permeated by the composer's national coloring and that it is Dvořák from start to finish. In a word, the man is greater than his subject matter. Individuality, like blood, will tell." These comments undercut nearly all of Dvořák's previous statements, especially his insistence that "negro melodies" were distinctly American.[37]

The New York press continued to push Dvořák for more insight as the premiere of his symphony drew closer. Although he had remained silent about racial issues over the summer, the *Evening Post* got him to talk in a late September interview. "I have been misunderstood in this connection," he said, referring specifically to "negro melodies." "What matters it to me if the best negro melodies have been written by white men?" The music's historical and emotional ties to Black bodies, it turns out, had not informed his opinions about its potential as a truly American source of inspiration. Rather, he perceived "negro melodies" as inert musical material simply awaiting his manipulation—as absolute music. After all, he had arranged Stephen Foster's "Old Folks at Home" for an all-Black choir featuring Sissieretta Jones and Harry T. Burleigh as soloists in Carnegie Hall—a collection of Black voices and Black bodies performing the work of two white men who freely appropriated the sounds of Black music.[38]

NOTES

1. "Dvořák Leads for the Fund," *NYH*, 24 Jan. 1894.
2. Dwight, "Mr. Fry and His Critics," *DJM*, 4 Feb. 1854, 141–42; Wilson, "A Chronicle," *BMH*, July 1892, 147.
3. Gleason, "American Composers," *AAJ*, 3 Oct. 1891, 398.
4. Gilchrist, "Is There to Be a Distinctive American School of Music?" *AAJ*, 16 Apr. 1892 (orig. 22 Aug. 1885), 11.
5. "A Letter from E.A. M'Dowell," *MC*, 10 Aug 1892, 6.

6. Higginson, "Negro Spirituals," *Atlantic Monthly*, June 1867, 685–94.
7. Huneker, "Dvořák's New Symphony," *MC*, 20 Dec. 1893, 37–38; Johann Tonsor [Mildred Hill], "Negro Music," *Music*, Dec. 1892, 119–22.
8. "In the Dramatic World," *NYW*, 23 June 1893.
9. Kramer, "Harry T. Burleigh," *MA*, 29 Apr. 1916, 25.
10. Dvořák to Thomas, 14 Apr. 1893, TTP.
11. Dvořák quoted in Otakar Šourek, *Antonin Dvořák: Letters and Reminiscences*, trans. Roberta Finlayson Samsour (New York: Da Capo Press, 1985), 152.
12. "Real Value of Negro Melodies," *NYH*, 21 May 1893.
13. Beckerman, *New Worlds*, 99–110.
14. "Negro Melody and American Composers," *NYH*, 6 June 1893; Beckerman, *New Worlds*, 102–3.
15. "American Music," *NYHE*, 26 May 1893; "Herr Rubinstein is Sceptical," *NYHE*, 27 May 1893; "America's Musical Future," *NYHE*, 28 May 1893.
16. See, for example, Rebecca J. Scott, "The Atlantic World and the Road to *Plessy v. Ferguson*," *Journal of American History* (2007): 726–33; Helen Heran Jun, *The Race to Citizenship: Black Orientalism and Asian Uplift from Pre-Emancipation to Neoliberal America* (New York: New York University Press, 2011), 15–31; Stephen G. Hall, *A Faithful Account of the Race: African American Historical Writing in Nineteenth-Century America* (Chapel Hill: University of North Carolina Press, 2009), 151–87.
17. "American Music," *BH*, 28 May 1893.
18. "American Music," *BH*, 28 May 1893.
19. "Criticisms on Dvořák's Theory," *NYH*, 4 June 1893.
20. "Musical and Dramatic Gossip," *Freund's Weekly*, 1 July 1893, 4.
21. "Negro Song Writers," *NYH*, 18 June 1893.
22. Ibid.
23. "The Foundations of Art," *New Orleans Daily Picayune*, 4 June 1893.
24. See Ronald Radano, *Lying Up a Nation: Race and Black Music* (Chicago: University of Chicago Press, 2003), 146–48.
25. "American Music," *BH*, 28 May 1893.
26. "In the World of Music," *NYW*, 4 June 1893.
27. "Dvořák and Folk-Song," *BDA*, 2 June 1893.
28. "A Reply to Dvořák and His Negro Melodies," *AAJ*, 17 June 1893, 224.
29. "American Music," *BH*, 28 May 1893.
30. "Nationalism in Music," *MC*, 14 June 1893, 7.
31. "American Music," *BH*, 28 May 1893.
32. "Negro Songs Rich in Melody," *NYH*, 2 July 1893.
33. "Criticisms of Dvořák's Theory," *NYH*, 4 June 1893.
34. "Herr Rubinstein is Sceptical," *NYHE*, 27 May 1893; "American Music," *BH*, 28 May 1893.
35. "For National Music," *ChiTr*, 13 Aug. 1893.

36 "Musical Matters," *NYTr*, 17 Sep. 1893.
37 "Last Sunday's Tribune," *MC*, 20 Sep 1893, 7.
38 "Dr. Dvořák's Year in America," *NYEP*, 30 Sep. 1893; see also Deane L. Root, "The Stephen Foster–Antonín Dvořák Connection," in *Dvořák in America, 1892–1895*, ed. John C. Tibbetts (Portland, OR: Amadeus Press, 1993), 243–54.

CHAPTER 7
THE RACIAL CHALLENGE

August 25, 1893—Chicago

Black Americans from all over the country streamed to Chicago for a day at the World's Columbian Exposition designed to highlight Black cultural achievement. After a morning parade through the city, attendees settled onto the fairgrounds and found their seats at the Festival Hall in the afternoon (see figure 7.1).

At 3:00 p.m., Frederick Douglass stood and delivered a stern but fiery message. "We hear nowadays of a frightful something called a negro problem. There is, in fact, no such problem. The real problem has been given a false name. It is called negro for a purpose. It has substituted negro for Nation, because the one is despised and hated, and the other is loved and honored. The true problem is a National problem." The energized crowd erupted in applause after nearly every sentence.

Once the crowd settled, the program continued with arias sung by tenors J. Arthur Freeman and Sidney Woodward and a poem recited by Paul Laurence Dunbar. An event manager apologized that famed soprano Sissieretta Jones couldn't appear, but mezzo Desseria Plato took her place. The concert closed with an elocution by Hattie Q. Brown and some numbers on the violin presented by Douglass's grandson, Joseph.

As they left, no one could forget Douglass's words. "Those who find politics in Mr. Douglass' speech," a writer for the *Inter Ocean* observed, "might be charged with putting it there themselves, because of their own consciousness as to why the race question touches politics."[1]

The 1893 World's Columbian Exposition in Chicago marking the four hundredth anniversary of Christopher Columbus's arrival on American shores was one of the century's most ostentatious cultural events to date. Divided into two

COLORED AMERICAN DAY AT FESTIVAL HALL.

FIGURE 7.1. Cartoon of World's Fair, *Daily Inter Ocean* (Chicago), 26 Aug. 1893.

sections—the White City, a series of buildings showcasing American excellence, and the Midway Plaisance, a park lined with exhibits displaying various world cultures—the fair was also a powerful metaphor of post-Reconstruction society. The fair's commissioners relegated Chinese Americans to the Midway Plaisance, for example, compelling them to find a balance between displaying "authentic" Chinese culture and asserting their identity as Americans.[2]

Black Americans, meanwhile, also had no seat on the 208-person board of commissioners, which made few provisions for their inclusion as part of the American-focused exhibits or as employees. Even after a "Jubilee Day," or "Colored American Day," was placed on the calendar, Black intellectuals and journalists, including antilynching activist Ida B. Wells, rejected the idea as tokenism. It would simply become an opportunity for visitors to believe that the all-white commissioners had "permitted" African Americans to have a special day, she argued, rather than to witness Black contributions to all facets of American society. Wells, Frederick Douglass, and others had called for a general boycott of the fair, but Douglass eventually relented and used his appearance at the fair to draw attention to American hypocrisy toward African American citizens.[3]

In the months leading up to Dvořák's arrival in September 1892, Will Marion Cook, a young Black violinist and composer (see figure 7.2), had begun writing an opera based on Harriet Beecher Stowe's *Uncle Tom's Cabin*. With the support of luminaries like Frederick Douglass, Cook sought permission from President Benjamin Harrison to stage musical events at the fair, arguing that Black Americans hadn't been part of the planning process but deserved at least some leadership roles. According to his plan, the opera production would feature an all-Black cast, including the famous soprano Sissieretta Jones, while other Black performers would participate in a variety of other events throughout the six months of the fair (see figure 7.3). "In this way," he wrote in a letter to the *Detroit Plaindealer*,

FIGURE 7.2. Will Marion Cook (1869–1944). Courtesy Music Division, New York Public Library for the Performing Arts.

"the great progress and ability of the Negro can be seen and better appreciated."[4]

By January 1893, Cook had secured tentative participation from several soloists, including Jones and baritone Harry T. Burleigh, as well as a small choir. But he needed money. Douglass gave him $1,000 when the opera was finished, with the understanding that Cook would also seek help elsewhere. To that end, he asked Jones to headline a fundraising concert at Carnegie's Music Hall in February, which would be the first appearance of Black artists at the venue (see figure 7.3). He also asked none other than Jeannette Thurber for practical assistance. Thurber, of

FIGURE 7.3. Matilda Sissieretta Joyner Jones (1868–1933). Courtesy Schomburg Center for Research in Black Culture, Manuscripts, Archives and Rare Books Division, The New York Public Library.

course, had long dreamed of a truly American opera and leaped at the chance to support Cook's project. Enchanted by the idea, she introduced him to several wealthy patrons who bought tickets to the concert. Douglass himself opened with an oration, while the vocal soloists performed European and American arias, conservatory piano student Paul Bolin played a polonaise by Ignace Jan Paderewski, Cook accompanied Jones on violin, and the choir closed with a rendition of "Swing Low, Sweet Chariot."[5]

A few weeks later, Thurber received a letter from a Black vocalist in Richmond that prompted her to announce that the National Conservatory would open its doors to talented Black students free of charge. The author, Fanny Payne Walker, lamented that she couldn't pursue a musical education after being widowed with two young children. But Sissieretta Jones had heard her sing and insisted that she write to Thurber to ask for admission to the school. "I have had lots to contend with indeed," Walker explained, but had no relatives who could help. "I have always craved for music and I love it." Thurber decided that the best way to help talented Black musicians like Walker was to prepare them at the conservatory to be professors—a noble effort but perhaps also an attempt to draw pupils away from competitors like the New England Conservatory or successful all-Black programs like those at Fisk and the Hampton Institute.[6]

To start, Thurber appointed students Harry T. Burleigh and Paul Bolin to the voice and piano faculties, while Dvořák appointed Walter F. Craig, a well-known local Black professional conductor and violinist, as a member to augment the student orchestra. These gestures inspired Bolin's brother, New York attorney Gaius C. Bolin, to write a letter

FIGURE 7.4. Program for World's Fair Colored Opera Company Benefit, 13 Feb. 1893. Courtesy Carnegie Hall Archives.

to the *New York Herald* explaining why the new policy was so valuable for African Americans:

> Amid the many discouragements which come to the colored people of this country in this fierce struggle for existence, and

in which they are so greatly and so very unjustly handicapped, there does come to them occasionally a ray of hope and great encouragement when they find those who are broad minded, liberal viewed, and humane enough to consider and truly feel that no matter what the color of a man's skin, no matter what the place or condition of his birth, he is a man, endowed with all the attributes of man, and that he stands before the just law and before his Maker as significant and as precious as any other human being.[7]

Bolin, the first Black graduate of Williams College, had experienced this "great encouragement" firsthand, not only during his student days, but when a generous lawyer in his hometown of Poughkeepsie, New York, allowed him to study law and sit for the bar exam. He passed the exam three months after Dvořák arrived.[8]

Dvořák himself also played a role in Thurber's decision to admit Black students free of charge. In a letter appearing alongside Bolin's, he expressed his deep sympathy for the policy because he, too, had experienced economic struggle firsthand. "It is to the poor that I turn for musical greatness," he wrote, because "the poor work hard; they study seriously. Rich people are apt to apply themselves lightly to music, and to abandon the painful toll to which every strong musician must submit without complaint and without rest." He then attributed his own success to the fact that his economic hardships had forced him to struggle. Although he didn't mean for his sympathetic comments to draw special attention to racial politics, their proximity to Bolin's letter united his ideas to the daily struggles of African Americans. At the same time, his easy conflation of economic and racial oppression failed to convey that the exclusion of nonwhite people from certain facets of public life knew no class boundaries.[9]

A NEW THREAD

The conservatory's new policy was announced in the same article in which Dvořák suggested that "negro melodies" should become the foundation of an American compositional school. Most participants in the ensuing debate, including Dvořák himself, addressed questions about musical style as if they were merely technical. But several others focused on the direct relationship between Dvořák's ideas and concrete race relations. Chicago music theorist A. J. Goodrich, for example, explained that "Americans have been loth [sic] to dignify the melodies of the negroes who were brought here and forced into slavery." But these melodies, he explained, which "belong to the American negro," are "the folk songs of this country." Pointing to the popular success of the Fisk Jubilee Singers, he urged composers to "learn not to despise that which touches the hearts of the people because it is of lowly origin" and commended the conservatory for its decision to support Black students. "It will give one more even chance to the negroes to compete with the whites in one of the greatest arts of civilization."[10]

A week later, Harry C. Smith, editor of the *Cleveland Gazette*, became one of few Black intellectuals to weigh in on the subject publicly and joined Goodrich in his support of Dvořák's ideas. Smith pointed out that these ideas had been "a bitter pill indeed for many prejudiced musicians (white) to swallow." Dvořák, he argued, "is on the right track, for the simple reason that about all the truly American music we have is furnished in these very same 'Negro' melodies." Smith explained that this music had been "*the* secret" for the success of the Fisk Jubilee Singers in Europe, while white Americans "had been too busy since the birth of this republic borrowing from the works of foreigners." As far as he was concerned, it would be "absolutely necessary that the folksongs furnished by our people while in the toils of slavery be drawn upon" for a distinctively American style.[11]

Smith and Goodrich were echoing sentiments that had accrued to the Fisk Jubilee Singers and their emulators for two decades. After an 1873 performance by the Hampton Institute Singers, for example, the *New York Weekly Review* described the music they performed as "our only native American music." A few years later, Black music historian James Monroe Trotter called this repertoire "our only distinctive *American* music" and believed that anyone listening to jubilee singers would admit that "in these 'slave-songs' of the South was to be found a new musical idea, forming, as some are wont to term it, a '*revelation*.'" And even a German critic had reached the same conclusion after hearing the Fisk Jubilee Singers in Berlin. If Liszt and Brahms could make Hungarian music accessible to Germans, he wondered, "could an apostle with energy and zeal for Negro music give it a similar place in our musical life?"[12]

After reading Dvořák's statements in the *New York Herald*, a writer for the *Baltimore Sun* wondered *who* exactly would "write us oratorios, symphonies, sonatas, and operas in the African style." For this writer, the apostle's identity was clear: "We shall unquestionably have to ask our colored musicians, by study and application, to develop the principles of negro melody and give us a true negro opera." And the reason why no such person had emerged yet was just as clear: Black Americans' lack of access to musical education.

> It is only in the parts of the musical art that require patient study, broad grasp of principles, and severe practice that they are wanting, and this deficiency may be due largely to the fact that our colored citizens have only recently begun to be students in any branch of learning.[13]

A respected Black schoolteacher from Washington, DC, named Walter B. Hayson agreed, remarking that "the only lasting satisfaction can be in knowing that some talented, trained musician of our own has shared in immortalizing these only real folksongs in America." Thurber, of course, hoped to help the situation by opening the conservatory to Black students free of charge, enabling Dvořák's ideas about style to unite with the conservatory's educational and philanthropic mission.[14]

The director of the Hampton Institute Singers, F. G. Rathbun, wrote to the *Herald* a few weeks later to explain that achieving Dvořák's ideal was a difficult proposition because the spirituals were losing the meaning they held for earlier generations. "Even now," he said, "the younger generation of colored singers do not give them with the effectiveness that the 'old timers' did, and the reason, of course, is that the old people made them the expression of their joys and sorrows, their hopes and fears, and these hymns or spirituals were part of their very being." He feared the songs might lose this sense when "rendered into instruments" and suggested that teaching them with historical accuracy would allow composers to use them without allowing their music to sound like minstrel songs. Rathbun quoted his predecessor at Hampton, Thomas P. Fenner, to bring the point home: "It may be that this people which has developed such a wonderful musical sense in its degradation will, in its maturity, produce a composer who could bring a music of the future out of this music of the past."[15]

Could this composer be Will Marion Cook with his *Uncle Tom's Cabin* opera? The *New York Press* reported in June that Cook had "gathered in all of the songs of this nature," and transformed them into arias for the show. According to the story, Dvořák himself had "praised them highly and said that they are in line with his own ideas." Like Thurber, Dvořák believed that opera was the best conduit for national musical expression because it allows for greater freedom of expression than restrictive genres like the symphony. The day after Dvořák celebrated Bohemian Day at the World's Fair in Chicago, Harry Burleigh wrote him a letter reminding him that Cook had composed an opera and that he was set to play the lead baritone role. Taking Burleigh at his word, Dvořák accepted Cook into his composition studio for the fall term, and the stage was set for him to be the conservatory's most prized composition pupil.[16]

THE PREMIERE

As the winter concert season opened in 1893, a Czech American lawyer named Josef Jiří Král wrote an essay for a major music magazine that attempted to extract Dvořák from racial politics altogether. Responding to concerns that Dvořák's ideas about "negro melodies" would cause the American public too much distress about their history given how the debate had unfolded over the past few months, Král argued that "no American except, perhaps, a bloody shirt orator, recalls those disgraceful political conditions with pleasure." The melodies, he explained, "are not encomiums upon slavery," nor do they "call forth the shades of the Confederacy." Dvořák was "an absolute musician who reduces to music whatever *he* touches—not what touches *him*." The public evidently had nothing to worry about.[17]

The New York press, meanwhile, circulated the Philharmonic program annotations in early December, revealing that Dvořák had also studied Native American melodies and written the inner movements "under the influence of Longfellow's *Song of Hiawatha*." This fact marked a significant departure from public expectations earlier in the year. On the morning of the Philharmonic's open rehearsal, the press also competed for the best original coverage. The *Herald* provided an exclusive interview while Henry Krehbiel wrote an exhaustive analysis for the *Tribune*, both of which challenged Král's fixation on absolute music. In the *Herald* interview, for example, Dvořák claimed that the second movement was a "study" for an opera or cantata based on Longfellow's poem while the third "was suggested" by Hiawatha's wedding feast. If these reports were correct, nationalists and everyone along the aesthetic divide could find something to savor in equal measure, with only universalists like Král left in the lurch.[18]

Although the audience at the first rehearsal responded with unhinged enthusiasm (see figure 7.5), critical responses to the symphony were mixed. Composer Reginald De Koven, who had expressed doubts about the national representativeness of "negro melodies" earlier in the year, remained skeptical:

> Whether [the symphony] will be accepted as characteristically national in the spirit of the composer's meaning and purpose, or whether, indeed, negro or Indian melodies, or imitations or reproductions of them, however clever or scientific, can justly be considered as representing national musical thought, are questions which can hardly be discussed here.[19]

Conductor Walter Damrosch agreed, saying "it suggests nothing American." And yet the audience had screamed for

FIGURE 7.5. Cartoon of New World Symphony Premiere, *New York Herald*, 16 Dec. 1893.

more: "Were they not justified in regarding this composition, the first fruits of Dr. Dvořák's musical genius since his residence in this country, as a distinctly American work of art?"[20]

Closing the year's sensationalist loop, the *Herald* also ran two more stories on the morning after the official premiere. One took credit for the work's immediate public success with the egregiously false claim that Dvořák had written the symphony "in consequence of the famous controversy aroused by a series of articles in the *Herald*." In a more careful review, critic Albert Steinberg considered the piece an artistic triumph:

> As Dr. Dvořák has said, the symphony has been inspired by a close study of the native melodies of the North American Indians and the negro race of this country. This study results in the discovery that in all essential particulars the national music of the two races is identical. [. . .] Following the principles which Brahms, Liszt, Schubert, and even Haydn have followed in certain of their compositions, Dr. Dvořák made the spirit of this savage music his own.[21]

Krehbiel's vision of Dvořák as the symphonist of the future, capable of transcending all artistic boundaries, had evidently become a reality in Steinberg's mind, though the precise language of his review illustrated the widespread belief that music created by nonwhite people could be collapsed into an exotic monolith with no unique cultural resonance.[22]

Krehbiel himself agreed with Steinberg's assessment. Recalling the controversy raging over the previous several months, he explained that some critics had been "sitting in their tubs of self-satisfied wisdom" and "asserted that all good music is universal and nationalism is a figment of the imagination." Others, he added, had used openly racist justifications for insulting Dvořák and his ideas. "But while these wise men were talking, Dvořák was listening with ears of genius, and before they got through, he had written his new symphony." Krehbiel warned, though, that the controversy would be far from over:

> It will be easy to say that it is a beautiful symphony, but that its character is not distinctively American. Some will call it a Celtic symphony, and they will not have to go far for arguments. [...] All that it is necessary to admit is the one thing for which he has compelled recognition—that there are musical elements in America that lend themselves to beautiful treatment in the higher forms of the art.[23]

And he was right. The symphony itself would set off another firestorm as vicious as the first.

THE SECOND STORM

Steinberg's and Krehbiel's reviews focused on the technical aspects of Dvořák's efforts to infuse his music with an American national spirit. But other commentators returned to questions of racial politics that had animated the debate before the premiere: the origins of Black music and the extent to which it could be considered American at all. Echoing Harry Smith of the *Cleveland Gazette*, several critics argued in favor of the authentic Americanness of "negro melodies" and their use in Dvořák's symphony. W. J.

Henderson of the *Times*, who had remained relatively quiet during the summertime debate, now gave a forceful assent:

> Our South is ours. Its twin does not exist. Our system of slavery, with all its domestic and racial conditions was ours. Its twin does not exist. Out of the heart of this slavery, environed by this sweet and languorous South, from the canebrake and the cotton field, arose the spontaneous musical utterance of a people. [. . .] If these songs are not national, there is no such thing as national song.[24]

Predictably, some people disagreed—and strongly. The mercurial Nym Crinkle, for example, presented a twisted history to make the opposite case:

> However characteristic the plantation melodies may be (and no doubt in their best form they served as a sort of folk song), they were the outcome of slavery and not of Americanism. In fact, in just so far as they were the expression of the pathos of servitude they were un-American. That they were is historically shown in the fact that the war killed the plantation song and wiped out of existence the ballad form of music known to us as "negro minstrelsy."[25]

Dismissing the piece's musical origins entirely, Crinkle felt that Dvořák would have been better off giving "tonal expression to Il Capitan [*sic*]" and harmonizing "the rush of Niagara and the long-drawn sighs of the Mammoth Cave. Now that is American."[26]

James Huneker of the *Musical Courier* was also having none of it. None: "His new symphony in E minor is not American." Mocking Krehbiel's prediction, Huneker went on to explain that "the most marked theme of the first movement is Celtic in quality, and it reappears in every movement of the work." The second movement? "Certainly not American." The third? "Sclavic [*sic*] and eminently Dvořákian." The finale? "It may be American but it sounds very Celtic or very Scandinavian." The American symphony, he lamented, "has yet to be written."[27]

Someone at the *Courier*, possibly Huneker, kept going the following week, this time singling out Krehbiel by name and denying Black music's "citizenship" in the country's musical landscape:

> Admitting for the sake of argument that negro melodies are indigenous to the Southern soil, why should this melodic product of a once enslaved people be considered the type of an American school?
>
> Negro melodies are nothing but old Spanish and French melodies transmogrified into the peculiar dialect of the slave, just as southern French and Spanish became the curious so-called creole "patois" that it is to-day.
>
> A sort of "brogue" is negro music, and all attempts to dignify it as a language are futile. Its roots are un-American. [. . .] Much of it was written by white men like Stephen Foster, who felt the sadness and after sweetness of it; but that such a genre should stand for the country as a whole is ridiculous. [. . .] It is not American, however, and curiously enough neither is his E minor symphony. It is more Celtic and Slavic than even negro.[28]

Comments like these, which twisted history for plainly racist ends, angered Chicago music theorist A. J. Goodrich, who had argued the opposite point at least twice in the past eighteen months:

> Of course there are Americans who are loth to acknowledge that the plantation melodies and rhythms are American; but the facts must be considered. [...] The edict of Lincoln, issued 30 years ago, broke every slave chain and destroyed every auction block in North America, and the plantation melody remains as a memory of that mighty struggle in which the brighter spirits of justice and freedom finally prevailed over oppression and disenfranchisement.[29]

For Huneker, however, "Little matter if the flowers he offers be those of the north, south, east, or west." He thought great music could rise above time, place, and certainly politics.

But questions like these certainly did matter. Two months after the premiere, a superintendent of a New Jersey electric lamp factory named G. Wilfred Pearce wrote a letter to the *New York Sun* again denying Black authorship of "negro melodies." The letter is filled with an extraordinarily detailed set of "facts" allegedly gleaned from personal research. He claimed, for example, that an Irish surgeon wrote one of the "negro melodies" Dvořák had used in the New World Symphony even though the doctor had never seen "the cane and cotton fields he writes and sings about in the music." Pearce went on to argue that contemporary African Americans wanted to deny their own ties to the past by seeking out white luxuries like "really good music by the masters."[30]

Although the *Sun* published a half-hearted anonymous rebuttal, Black schoolteacher Walter B. Hayson wrote an article for the *Cleveland Gazette* attacking Pearce's baseless comments:

> A short while ago, Dr. Antonín Dvořák made the assertion that a distinctive American school of music could be founded upon the Negro melodies of the south. This was at once a thrust, purposely or unintentionally, at the non-musicalness of the White American, and at the same time a recognition of, and a compliment to the musical nature of the Negro-American.
>
> Up to this time the Americans were perfectly satisfied that their composers, G. W. Chadwick, Buck, Foote, Paine, E. A. MacDowell, had ignored Negro melodies. But for a foreigner to dignify these "nigger minstrel songs," by using them as *motifs* and *themes* for symphonies, suites, and other high-class music, and that too as a foundation for an American school of music, was too much. They therefore hastened to discover that these Negro melodies were not *Negro* melodies after all.³¹

Hayson went on to dismantle Pearce's "facts" with surgical precision. An accurate history of the United States, he closed, would never record that "the white American, who stole away everything else from the slave, actually stopped at his songs and tunes." This music was too important to let racist narratives go unchallenged, because "they are our own and represent something. [. . .] They make up our folk-lore, the only intellectual inheritance our enslaved forefathers have left us." No one could take that away.³²

Dvořák never realized that his ideas, much less his music, would expose the deep wounds of racism in American society. Betraying his ignorance, he told the *New York Press* in October 1893 that "what I said has already aroused not race prejudice so much as musical prejudice." And despite all that Dvořák had done to improve the lives of Black musicians by accepting them into the conservatory, his student Will Marion Cook perceived Dvořák's ignorance of racial dynamics in the symphony itself. Calling the piece "a great triumph, which was, paradoxically a failure," he explained in an 1898 reflective essay:

> Faithful as was his insight into the character of the Negro—now light, now heavy, now gay, now sad—yet something lacked; that something, which even Dvořák's great genius failed to comprehend, and only a Negro who had seen and felt and suffered could supply.[33]

Although Cook failed to produce *Uncle Tom's Cabin* at the Columbian Exposition—or ever—he remained optimistic. "And who knows?" he asked, "Soon perhaps will some native composer, hopeful of the future, take the pen, and inspired by long repressed imagination, paint glowing tone pictures of a radiant dawn—a dawn without a passing—a day without a night." In other words, Cook knew that Dvořák's appropriation of Black music was at best a single step toward racial justice and that only placing nonwhite composers on an equal footing would enable the landscape of classical music in the United States to reflect American ideals.[34]

NOTES

1. "Colored People's Day," *DIO*, 27 Aug. 1893.
2. Yuki Ooi, "'China' on Display at the Chicago World's Fair of 1893: Faces of Modernization in the Contact Zone," in *From Early Tang Court Debates to China's Peaceful Rise*, ed. Friederike Assandri and Dora Martins (Amsterdam: Amsterdam University Press, 2009), 53–66.
3. "That 'Jubilee Day,'" *The Freeman*, 18 Mar. 1893; Anna R. Paddon and Sally Turner, "African Americans and the World's Columbian Exposition," *Illinois Historical Journal* 88 (1995): 19–36.

4 "Colored Singers at the World's Fair," *WaPo*, 17 Oct. 1892; "A Novel Idea," *Detroit Plaindealer*, 21 Oct. 1892.
5 "A Great Scheme," *CG*, 21 Jan. 1893; "New Opera by a Negro, about Negroes, and to be Sung by Negroes," *NYW*, 12 Feb. 1893; John Graziano, "The Early Life and Career of 'the Black Patti': The Odyssey of an African American Singer in the Late Nineteenth Century," *Journal of the American Musicological Society* 53 (2000): 574–75.
6 "Real Value of Negro Melodies," *NYH*, 21 May 1893.
7 "Antonín Dvořák on Negro Melodies," *NYH*, 28 May 1893; Loomis, "Gaius C. Bolin," *Williams Magazine* (Spring 2016): 29–31.
8 "Mr. Walter F. Craig," *Detroit Plaindealer*, 13 Jan. 1893.
9 "Antonín Dvořák on Negro Melodies," *NYH*, 28 May 1893; see also Jacqueline M. Moore, *Leading the Race: The Transformation of the Black Elite in the Nation's Capital, 1880–1920* (Charlottesville: University Press of Virginia, 1999).
10 "American Melodies," *DIO*, 28 May 1893.
11 "Dr. Dvořák on the Right Track," *CG*, 3 June 1893.
12 "The Hampton Singers," *New York Weekly Review*, 22 Mar. 1873, 1; James Monroe Trotter, *Music and Some Highly Musical People* (Boston: Lee and Shepard, 1880), 324; Langhans, "Die Jubiläumssänger," *Neue Berliner Musikzeitung*, 15 Nov. 1877, 363 (my translation); see also Sandra Jean Graham, *Spirituals and the Birth of a Black Entertainment Industry* (Urbana: University of Illinois Press, 2018), 1–81.
13 "An African School of Music," *Baltimore Sun*, 3 June 1893.
14 "Music Galore," *Cleveland Gazette*, 16 Dec. 1893.
15 "Negro Songs Rich in Melody," *NYH*, 2 July 1893.
16 "*Uncle Tom* in Opera," *NYP*, 25 June 1893; "For National Music," *ChiTr*, 13 Aug. 1893; Burleigh to Dvořák, quoted in Maurice Peress, *Dvořák to Duke Ellington: A Conductor Explores America's Music and Its African American Roots* (New York: Oxford University Press, 2004), 31–32.
17 "Dr. Antonín Dvořák," *Music*, Oct. 1893, 566–69.
18 "Dvořák on His New Work," *NYH*, 15 Dec. 1893; "Dr. Dvořák's American Symphony," *NYTr*, 15 Dec. 1893; Beckerman, *New Worlds*, 23–65.
19 "Dvořák's Symphony," *NYW*, 16 Dec. 1893.
20 "Dr. Dvořák's Great Symphony," *NYH*, 16 Dec. 1893.
21 "Dvořák Hears His Symphony," *NYH*, 17 Dec. 1893.
22 "Dvořák's Symphony a Historic Event," *NYH*, 17 Dec. 1893.
23 "Dr. Dvořák's Symphony," *NYTr*, 17 Dec. 1893.
24 "Dr. Dvořák's Latest Work," *NYT*, 17 Dec. 1893; see also Stevenson "Music," *Indep*, 21 Dec. 1893, 10–11.
25 "Views and Reviews," *NYW*, 17 Dec. 1893.
26 Finck, "A Notable Concert," *NYEP*, 18 Dec. 1893.
27 "The Second Philharmonic Concert," *MC*, 20 Dec. 1893, 37–38.

28 "Why American?," *MC*, 27 Dec. 1893, 8–9.
29 "Is There a Basis for American Music?," *AAJ*, 6 Jan. 1894, 260.
30 "Negroes and Negro Melodies," *NYS*, 15 Feb. 1894.
31 "Negro Melodies," *CG*, 23 Apr. 1894.
32 See also "Negroes and Negro Melodies," *NYS*, 4 Mar. 1894.
33 "Music of the Negro," *Illinois Record*, 14 May 1898.
34 "Dvořák's Remarkable Assertion," *NYP*, 27 Oct. 1893.

CHAPTER 8
THE SPIRITUAL AFTERMATH

June 15, 1933—Chicago

The lovely warm evening couldn't keep music lovers from cramming into Auditorium Theatre for a Friends of Music program honoring the achievements of Black musicians, including Chicago's own Florence Price and Margaret Bonds. George Gershwin, who had dazzled the city the previous night, soaked in the view of the hall from fellow composer John Alden Carpenter's box.

At 8:15 p.m., conductor Frederick Stock strode onto the stage and waved to the brass section—What's that? A hint of "Dixie"? Much of the audience shuffled uncomfortably during

John Powell's pompous *In Old Virginia*. But it all faded when Roland Hayes walked on stage and began singing a Berlioz aria with that strong liquid tenor voice everyone knew and loved.

Florence Price's new symphony, a contest winner, combined old and new beauties—a hint of Dvořák but a voice all her own. The mood in the hall lightened at the sounds of a juba dance in the third movement, and a roar of applause compelled the composer to rise and be acknowledged. Hayes's soaring voice then pierced the hearts of everyone present in Samuel Coleridge-Taylor's "Onaway! Awake Beloved."

Bonds, musically mature far beyond her twenty years, walked quickly on stage and played Carpenter's lively concertino as if she had written it herself, eliciting a roaring ovation and six calls back to the stage.

Hayes returned to sing two spiritual arrangements that left the audience stunned into silence. Coleridge-Taylor's *Bamboula* wrenched everyone back into real world and lifted everyone out of their seats in a display of unbridled appreciation.

"As we listened to that concert," editor Robert Abbot wrote in the *Chicago Defender*, "we took hope yet again that there may yet be brotherhood in this land of ours."[1]

As the New World Symphony traveled to concert halls in every direction over the months and years after its premiere, Dvořák's presence left an indelible mark on the country's cultural landscape. The seeds of discussion that his music and ideas had planted—from ownership of the spirituals to the national identity of the symphony itself—continued to shape the lives of American musicians and music lovers for decades.[2]

ANTONÍN DVOŘÁK

Dvořák traveled home for the summer in 1894 before returning for his final year as conservatory director. By this time, he had already finished several new works, including the "American" string quartet, a string quintet, a violin sonatina, a piano suite, and the ill-fated patriotic cantata, *The American Flag*, which Thurber hoped would premiere at his welcome concert in 1892. He resumed a high level of activity upon his return in October and wrote the Cello Concerto, piano humoresques, and an essay for *Harper's Magazine*. After leaving the United States for good in 1895, he settled in Prague and eventually became director of the conservatory there. The cantata premiered just days after his departure, but it did not impress. Henry Finck wrote, "We must suspect that the enthusiasm aroused in the doctor's breast by Drake's poem was dampened by the sight of our flag itself, which, on account of its associations, may be a joy forever, but from an artistic and chromatic point of view is not a thing of beauty, being, in fact, almost as bad as our stamps."[3]

Dvořák's advocacy of Black vernacular music, acknowledgment of its authentic Americanness, and willingness to teach Black students of all backgrounds left a distinct positive impression on many of the country's Black classical musicians. In Washington, DC, for example, a music professor at Howard University named J. Henry Lewis founded an all-Black amateur group "for the purpose of inspiring the advanced or higher class of music" and called it the Dvořák Musical Society. In May 1900, the society staged a production of Gilbert and Sullivan's *Pirates of Penzance* that a Washington correspondent to the *Musical Courier* called "one of the best (if not the best) amateur opera performances of the season."[4]

Music critic Sylvester Russell wrote an impassioned eulogy for the *Indianapolis Freeman* in June 1904 that captured the iconic status the composer had achieved in certain Black musical circles:

> In his teachings we can all look back with pride to slavery—slavery's music—and the price the slaves paid to have their sweet echoes of agony, which touch every soul, re-echoed back to home by Him from abroad, and exclaim "bravo" to the Great Dvořák in life, "bravo" to him in death; for though he be dead, his death is a new life to his musical greatness and a living death forever.[5]

This hagiographic impulse quickly faded, but Dvořák's US residency remained noteworthy in Black musical historiography. Writing forty years apart, musicologists Maud Cuney-Hare (1936) and Eileen Southern (1977) both considered his engagement with Black students like Harry

T. Burleigh and Will Marion Cook a significant moment in the development of Black American musical life.[6]

THE NEW WORLD SYMPHONY

As the New World Symphony moved to other cities after its 1893 premiere, it continued to elicit a bizarrely fragrant potpourri of responses. Its multidimensional expressions of national identity and its ambiguous position along the aesthetic spectrum prompted listeners to hear it in vastly different ways, many of which reflected deeply racist sentiments:

> BOSTON: Yesterday's audience gave rapt attention to the performance of the symphony and waited, expectantly, for the appearance of melodies characteristic of America. It is fair to presume that these expectations were not generally fulfilled.[7]
>
> BROOKLYN: Perhaps he has incidentally been through Chinatown and has picked up a strain or two.[8]
>
> LONDON: We cannot see how the great Anglo-Saxon republic can be expected to adopt negro and Indian tunes as national melodies, but that is hardly a question for us to consider. The Symphony appeals to us as music simply.[9]
>
> PHILADELPHIA: If any in the audience expected to find it a sort of amplification or glorification of the "Go-down Pharaoh" and "Swing Low, Sweet Chariot" sort of thing, they must have been disappointed. The truth about the new symphony is that it is no more distinctively American than the B minor symphony of Schubert or Tchaikovsky's "Symphonie Pathétique."[10]
>
> CHICAGO: The gayety and sadness of mood, quick in succession with the negro temperaments, afford a picture of alternating happiness and despair [in the scherzo]. This has been

grasped. So also has the longing for release from slavery, the call of freedom, the eager questioning of that which seems beyond belief, and the climax of the civil war.[11]

CINCINNATI: The largo is another part in which the idea of the realities of the new world arises. The whole movement suggests New England. The brasses open with a few measures of regular cadence, like the rolling of waters.[12]

After the belated Viennese premiere, in February 1896, leading conservative critic Eduard Hanslick was impressed by the work's "erotic" rhythms and melodies. And, never one to avoid taking a jab at Wagnerians, he assured readers that it had none of the "sound effects in the manner of Young Germans."[13]

The symphony only gained in popularity after Dvořák's death in 1904 and has appeared on orchestral programs throughout the United States and Europe in virtually every concert season since. Program annotations, in fact, became one more battleground for debating the music's national identity. A 1907 program for Walter Damrosch's Symphony Society, for example, provided a mind-boggling xenophobic account of the finale reflecting white backlash toward East European and Asian immigration:

In the last movement the composer seems to be looking with astonishment and dismay at the confusion of nationalities pouring into this country. The Irish jig, the Italian tarantella, and the American (*sic*) tune of "Three Blind Mice" follow each other in mad confusion.[14]

Perhaps hoping to outdo this writer, Boston Symphony annotator Philip Hale went to great pains to explain why the work was not American but Czech and that Dvořák had not been inspired by Black vernacular music after all. "Yet some," he lamented, "will undoubtedly insist that the symphony 'From the New World' is based, for the most part, on negro themes, and that the future of American music rests on the use of Congo, North American Indian, Creole, Greaser and cowboy ditties, whinings, yawps, and whoopings"—a clear echo of the white supremacist rhetoric that had driven the debates surrounding the symphony's premiere. (W. J. Henderson later refuted Hale in the *New York Sun*.) Meanwhile, arrangements of the Largo theme became staples on wind band concerts and pipe organ recitals around the world.[15]

ELLSWORTH PHELPS AND GEORGE FREDERICK BRISTOW

New York–based composers Ellsworth Phelps and George Frederick Bristow, distinguished figures in American music for decades, had a bone to pick with Dvořák after the New World Symphony premiere: He had taken their idea. After reading a few reviews, Phelps wrote a furious letter to the *Brooklyn Daily Eagle* to insist that credit be given where due:

> Our young critics seem to be oblivious to American musical history. It is probably regarded as a barren field. It is said that this symphony is the first instance of the use of native themes for symphonic purposes. In 1878 I gave the "Hiawatha" symphony in Brooklyn. [. . .] I did not try to produce the Indian in war paint and scalping knife, but simply the spirit of the poem. Later I gave the Emancipation symphony, producing necessarily the negro element after the same manner.[16]

A writer for the *Eagle* agreed, remarking after the symphony's Brooklyn premiere that "the name of E. C. Phelps will at once occur to every local music student and listener" in connection with American symphonies. Even so, Phelps fell into relative obscurity and died twenty years later at the end of a thirty-eight-year career teaching in the city's public schools.[17]

Bristow had also written two American symphonies—one from the 1870s depicting a wagon train's westward journey and one called "Niagara," which he had finished not long after Dvořák's arrival. In the middle of the debate in the summer of 1893, Bristow had told the *Musical Courier* that he thought Gottschalk would have done more for an American school had he lived longer and that his own new symphony contained a "walk about" on the antebellum parlor song "Near the Lake Where Drooped the Willow." But the national identity of the symphony fully emerges in the finale, where orchestra, chorus, and soloists join to sing praises for the natural beauty of Niagara Falls. The symphony premiered in Carnegie Hall a few months before Bristow died in a school classroom in December 1898.[18]

JEANNETTE THURBER AND THE NATIONAL CONSERVATORY

Jeannette Thurber's desire to support Black students persisted beyond Dvořák's tenure. The *New York Sun* reported in January 1894 that Dvořák had taken a special interest in Black voice students, believing that "in volume their voice is superior to whites, and in timbre it is equal if not superior." Echoing this biological essentialism, Thurber added, "I do not see why they could not be trained to opera as well as the Italian singers are. If, untrained, their voices are so excellent, what may we not expect after years of hard work and training?" A few months after Dvořák's departure, Thurber told the *New York Age*, a Black newspaper, that she was so impressed with Dvořák's ideas that she wanted to open a separate branch of the conservatory dedicated to "the encouragement and study of negro music" with an all-Black faculty and student body. This idea never got off the ground, but in 1903, Harriet Gibbs Marshall, the first Black woman to graduate from the Oberlin Conservatory, opened an all-Black conservatory in Washington, DC, where Thurber had once tried to move the National Conservatory.[19]

The National Conservatory itself declined steadily after Dvořák's departure. Its two subsequent directors, conductor Emil Paur and pianist Vasily Safonov, could not maintain its vibrance despite their sound international reputations. On the one hand, it faced direct competition from other private New York conservatories like Frank Damrosch's Institute for Musical Art. On the other, rising anti-European sentiment during the First World War prompted the introduction of a new congressional bill to establish a truly government-sponsored national conservatory. Thurber tried to leverage her national charter in 1921 by reorganizing the board with congressional approval. But she was never able to overcome mounting external challenges, especially after the Juilliard Graduate School, founded in 1924, merged with the Institute of Musical Art two years later. Thurber died in 1946 at the age of ninety-five.[20]

WILL MARION COOK AND HARRY T. BURLEIGH

After leaving Dvořák's composition studio, Will Marion Cook pivoted to the commercial music industry, first by publishing standalone songs and then by providing scores for musical theater shows. Although Cook acknowledged difficulties transitioning away from his classical training, his interactions with other intellectuals in the friendlier space of the Black theater, such as Paul Laurence Dunbar, James Weldon Johnson, and J. Rosamund Johnson, proved instrumental in his musical development. His theatrical collaborations with Dunbar, *Clorindy* and *In Dahomey*, were also two of the first all-Black productions on Broadway.

Cook spent much of his career directing or participating in ensembles designed to cultivate a uniquely Black musical aesthetic, including James Reese Europe's Clef Club and the Southern Syncopated Orchestra, which performed throughout Europe after the First World War. Perhaps remembering the debates surrounding Dvořák's ideas, he also fought against white denials of Black musical authorship. "Too long has this exploitation of Negro bodies and talent by white men seeking the limelight been tolerated," he wrote in 1927, "LET MY PEOPLE GO!" He died in 1944.[21]

Harry T. Burleigh launched a professional singing career well before Dvořák left. He had joined the posh St. George's Episcopal Church choir roster as baritone soloist in 1894 and continued to be in high demand as a recitalist through the 1920s. Although he had not studied composition with Dvořák, he published dozens of original works over the course of his long career. But Burleigh became known primarily as an arranger of spirituals and an advocate of their performance on the concert stage. After he met tenor Roland Hayes in 1912, Hayes championed his solo arrangements and helped establish the practice of including spirituals on recital programs alongside a variety of arias and art songs.[22]

Like Cook, Burleigh was also commercially savvy. As an editor for publisher G. Ricordi, he became one of two Black charter members of ASCAP in 1914 along with James Weldon Johnson, whose 1925 collection of spirituals became a touchstone in the Harlem Renaissance. But a white Dvořák student, William Arms Fisher, overshadowed Burleigh's direct influence on the New World Symphony when he published an arrangement of the Largo theme with a text in Black dialect under the title "Goin' Home," which some later confused as Dvořák's inspiration. (Conveniently, Fisher was an editor at a competing firm, Oliver Ditson.) Hoping to capitalize on the growing demand for spiritual arrangements, Fisher also published his own collection in 1926. Fisher's preface credited Burleigh with introducing Dvořák to the repertoire, but Burleigh spent much of his career resisting claims that Dvořák's symphony was either strictly Bohemian or free of national character. Burleigh and Fisher died within a year of each other, in 1948 and 1949.[23]

JOHN BROEKHOVEN AND HENRY SCHOENEFELD

John Broekhoven's *Suite Creole* (1884) gained new momentum when John Philip Sousa commissioned a band arrangement that he premiered in 1910 and programmed throughout his next world tour. Broekhoven suddenly became one of the most widely heard American composers of his generation. After the First World War, he developed xenophobic inclinations and argued that for American music to thrive, "the influence of foreign elements disseminated in this country by alien artists, teachers, and propagandists should be checked." J. Fischer published his suite in 1929 hoping to entice high school groups. Broekhoven died the next year and the piece fell into obscurity.[24]

Henry Schoenefeld maintained an international reputation after Dvořák selected his *Rural Symphony* to win the National Conservatory's first composition contest in 1893. Perhaps seeking a warmer climate than Chicago could offer, Schoenefeld moved to Los Angeles in 1904, where he became a respected member of the music community as director of the award-winning choir for the city's German Turnverein. In 1913 he took over the directorship of the Los Angeles Woman's Orchestra, one of the oldest and largest women's instrumental ensembles in the country (see figure 8.1); he stepped down in 1929. His orchestral music, including the *Rural Symphony*, concertos for violin and cello, a rhapsody overture called *In the Sunny South*, and the famous suite remained in international circulation until his death in 1936.[25]

HENRY F. GILBERT

Boston composer Henry F. Gilbert, an avid collector and arranger of folksongs from around the world (see figure 8.2), became the leading white advocate for the use of

FIGURE 8.1. Henry Schoenefeld with Los Angeles Women's Orchestra, *Pacific Coast Musician*, Dec. 1913. Courtesy RIPM Retrospective Index to Music Periodicals, www.ripm.org.

"negro melodies" in the early years of the twentieth century. Gilbert had been studying with Edward MacDowell at the New England Conservatory when Dvořák was in New York and, like many Americans, found his ideas engrossing. "As I was naturally a lover of the Negro songs," Gilbert recalled in 1921, "I began to make sketches for compositions based on their peculiar musical color or suggestion." After dire financial circumstances forced Gilbert away from composition for several years, he wrote a series of large-scale works in this vein between 1903 and 1916: *Americanesque, Comedy Overture on Negro Themes, Negro Rhapsody,* and *The Dance in Place Congo*. These pieces drew melodic material

Henry F. Gilbert

FIGURE 8.2. Henry Gilbert, ca. 1918. Courtesy Wilson Music Library, Vanderbilt University.

from older published song collections, including those by Thomas Wentworth Higginson and George William Cable. John Broekhoven, of course, had transformed Cable's findings into his *Suite Creole* in 1884.[26]

Gilbert argued passionately for better institutional support of American composers. As early as 1906, he helped inaugurate a concert series sponsored by the New Music Society, which a group of musicians formed with the belief that "present conditions in the American world, so far as they govern native compositions, are hostile to the normal development of a vigorous creative art." He returned to this theme throughout his career and became increasingly xenophobic after the First World War. "Our symphony orchestras," he wrote in 1921, "are almost entirely conducted by European conductors—Germans, Frenchmen, Austrians, and Italians. These persons, although excellent musicians usually, have no understanding of, nor sympathetic interest in, the struggles of a composer like myself toward the ultimate creation of a national American music."[27]

Major orchestras around the country did, in fact, program Gilbert's music with some frequency, and nearly all of their conductors had been born in Europe. Even Franz Xavier Arens, who had conducted Schoenefeld's suite throughout Europe in 1892, performed Gilbert's *Negro Rhapsody* with his People's Symphony Orchestra of New York in 1913. Gilbert's pieces also tended to be very well received. An enthusiastic crowd called Gilbert to the stage after Josef Stránský and the New York Philharmonic performed his *Comedy Overture* in 1913. And a performance of the *Negro Rhapsody* at the Norfolk Music Festival the same year floored Olin Downes: "Better than all, and most valuable," he wrote in *Musical America*, "is the fact that a man is saying in all sincerity something of his own, in strictly his own way. How would it have impressed Whitman? Would he have said, 'I hear America singing?'"[28]

But the *Comedy Overture* had precisely the opposite effect on Lena James Holt, a critic for the *Chicago Defender*, one of the country's most important Black newspapers. After hearing the Chicago Symphony perform it under Frederick Stock, she was aghast:

> Personally, I am skeptical of American whites writing Negro music, for one has but to revert to the days when minstrelsy began to know why they imitated the Negro, and the subsequent desecration of his working and sorrow songs into the vulgar and jingoistic ragtime.
>
> The Negro and the Indian are being sacrificed on the altar of popularity by ambitious composers, and these two peoples should take up this phase of their cultural development and guard it jealously, for to them belong the honors, if they but work for them.
>
> If the Negro will seriously study composing as he has medicine, theology, painting, literature and other sciences and arts, I predict that within the next twenty years the music world will hail a black Wagner and call him master.[29]

Of course, several Black composers, including Will Marion Cook, had already studied composition at conservatories in New York, Boston, and elsewhere but had run into a distinct lack of support from the country's most prominent ensembles and conductors. Holt herself, who later went by Nora Douglas Holt, was the first Black American to earn a master's degree in composition and had written a *Rhapsody on Negro Themes* of her own. Gilbert died in 1928 while orchestras around the country continued to play his music.[30]

W. E. B. DU BOIS

The great statesman Frederick Douglass died just weeks before Dvořák left for Europe in 1895, prompting several Black intellectual leaders, including Paul Laurence Dunbar, Walter B. Hayson, and W. E. B. Du Bois, to establish the American Negro Academy two years later. Du Bois's 1897 essay for the *Atlantic Monthly*, in which he coined the famous phrase "double-consciousness," was one of the first fruits of their discourse. He argued that African Americans should foster "the traits and talents of the Negro [. . .] in order that someday, on American soil, two world races may give each to each those characteristics which both so sadly lack." But, he added, "we come not altogether empty-handed: there is today no true American music but the sweet wild melodies of the Negro slave." The national identity of this music—the very topic that had shaped the debates surrounding the New World Symphony—would become a leitmotif in Du Bois's 1903 book *The Souls of Black Folk*.[31]

After Du Bois founded *The Crisis* as the official magazine of the NAACP in 1910, he became a clearinghouse of information about African American music and used the magazine to amplify his ideas about the repertoire's national identity. The famous muckraker Upton Sinclair wrote Du Bois in 1914 asking for a "few passages from genuine negro slave songs, which embody protest against social injustice. [. . .] I do not mean necessarily things that are definitely socialistic, but things that have an economic implication." Du Bois sent him stanzas from "Oh! Freedom," "Fighting On," and "We'll Die in the Field." A reader from San Jose,

California, wrote Du Bois in 1923 lamenting the loss of interest in the spirituals among younger African Americans. "This is sad," she said, and "much to be deplored when we consider that America owes to the Negro race her only true folk-music, unique and wonderful, musically and spiritually." Du Bois replied that "we agree entirely with everything you have said."[32]

Du Bois's eyes must have lit up in 1926 when a young man from Sumter, South Carolina, named Gamewell Valentine alerted him to a conflict in the *Musical Courier* about William Arms Fisher's recently published collection of spirituals. A reviewer for the *Courier* had wondered why another collection was necessary when they were "the most worthless, futile, and tiresome of all things musical." An angry Valentine wrote to the editors to complain about the dismissive attitude:

> What did Dvořák see in them? Was his judgment any good? No American composers have written any greater music than he. Have they? What about our own William Arms Fisher, a worthy pupil and disciple of Dvořák? Would he waste his time over futile music?
>
> There are many bad spirituals and contrariwise many good ones. The good spirituals are absolutely serious and were intended to be so. Nothing is more obnoxious to an audience who understands the spirituals than to sing them in "costume." To singers who wish to sing spirituals in costume, I suggest that they allow their feet to be chained and hard lashes administered to the bare back with leather made of cow's hide while singing. This is the costume that the Negro wore at the time the spirituals were created, and it will assist the singer to get into the mood of the song.[33]

Du Bois gladly reprinted excerpts from the feud and thanked Valentine for his efforts. Seizing the opportunity for publicity, Fisher then wrote Du Bois and asked if he might be interested in reviewing the collection himself. He printed one a few months later.[34]

JOHN POWELL AND LAMAR STRINGFIELD

Composer and pianist John Powell premiered his first work for piano and orchestra, *Rhapsodie nègre*, at Carnegie Hall on the evening after Henry Gilbert's ballet, *The Dance in Place Congo*, premiered at the Metropolitan Opera House earlier in the afternoon. Conductor Modest Altschuler and the Russian Symphony Orchestra, a group that had helped sponsor Gilbert's short-lived New Music Society of America in 1906, provided the accompaniment. Critic Herbert Peyser was beside himself with enthusiasm in his review for *Musical America*, calling Powell "one of the foremost creative geniuses the country has produced." Regarding the work itself, he explained,

> [The composer] is profoundly versed in all the ramifications of the black man's musical lore in consequence of prolonged and intimate first-hand acquaintance. He has in the present work set forth "the development of the negro since the days when he was first brought from his native home, Africa," to embody in some form the impassioned, almost barbaric emotionalism of the race as it exemplifies itself in the frenzied auto-intoxication to be often noted in the fanatical methods of religious devotion among the more privileged classes.[35]

"There is a savage, almost brutal polyphonic climax," he observed, "yielding gradually to a more peaceable slow section reared on a lyrical phrase with Dvořákian loveliness."

Powell was also a fervent white supremacist who played a central role in the development of Virginia's Racial Integrity Act of 1924—a law that banned interracial marriage, enshrined the "one-drop rule," and emboldened the Nazi regime to pursue eugenics. A year earlier, Powell wrote an essay called "Music and the Nation" that attempted to bridge the gap between eugenics policy and musical style. Commenting on Dvořák's ideas, he thought it was "absurd to imagine that the negro idiom could ever give adequate expression to the soul of our race." For Powell, studying "Anglo-Saxon folksong" was the only path forward. "Familiarity with this noble inheritance," he argued, "would revive and confirm in ourselves those traditions and feelings which are the crown of our race, and make possible for us, not merely the inauguration of a Golden Age of National Art, but assure to us as well that supremest glory, a nationhood, unparalleled in the annals of all time." Powell died in 1963 and is buried along with twenty-eight Confederate generals at Hollywood Cemetery in Richmond.[36]

North Carolina–based conductor and composer Lamar Stringfield was far less political but manifested some of Powell's compositional ideas in orchestral works like *From the Southern Mountains* and *Moods of a Moonshiner*. Stringfield developed a strong career as a flutist in New York City before moving back to North Carolina in the mid-1920s, where he founded and directed the Works Progress Administration–financed North Carolina Symphony. His chef d'oeuvre was a piece called *The Legend of John Henry*, a "symphonic ballad" depicting the tragic story of a railroad steel driver in a contest with a machine drill. For his ideal performance of the piece, Stringfield wanted to program an all-Black chorus singing "Swing Low, Sweet Chariot" as an introduction to the full New World Symphony. Then a group of folk singers from the mountains would tell the story of John Henry before the orchestra would take up his symphonic reflection. This concert was his portrait of a fully segregated America—Black and white side by side. He died in 1958.[37]

WILLIAM DAWSON AND FLORENCE PRICE

Famed conductor Leopold Stokowski premiered William Dawson's *Negro Folk Symphony* with the Philadelphia Orchestra in November 1934. Dawson, a faculty member at the Tuskegee Institute (see figure 8.3), had earned national acclaim as director of the school's choir. Excited about a project he had been preparing for years, he notified friends all over the country about the event. Much to his delight, the crowd roared at every concert, making the piece a decided success. After hearing the radio broadcast, many of his friends responded with jubilation. The great Black soprano Lillian Evanti had been listening with her mother in Washington, DC, and wrote, "Stupendous. Unprecedented. Thrilling. [. . .] When we speak of Mahler and Sibelius, we say Dawson too." Black violinist and composer Clarence Cameron White, head of music at the Hampton Institute, told Dawson it should be "as popular as Dvořák's 'New World' Symphony."[38]

FIGURE 8.3. William Levi Dawson, ca. 1930. Photo by Gushiniere. Courtesy Department of Special Collections and University Archives, W. E. B. Du Bois Library, University of Massachusetts Amherst.

Critical responses also tended to be enthusiastic. Philosopher Alain Locke, a leader of the Harlem Renaissance, called it a significant step along "a path to the Negro musician as was pointed by Dvořák years ago." But, for some critics, the music's resemblance to Dvořák's was a weakness bordering on plagiarism. A writer for *Musical*

America summed up this sentiment, noting that "the influence of Dvořák is strong almost to the point of quotation, and when all is said and done, the Bohemian composer's symphony, From the New World, stands as the best symphony à la Nègre written to date." These accusations, particularly that the symphony was "well garbed in Caucasian dress," rightly upset Dawson. "Dvořák used Negro idioms," he told the *Pittsburgh Courier*, and "that is my language. It is the language of my ancestors, and my misfortune is that I was not born when that great writer came to America in search of material." If Dvořák could write a symphony inspired by Black music, why couldn't Dawson? The *Negro Folk Symphony* gathered dust until 1963, when Stokowski recorded a heavily revised version. Dawson died in 1990 after a distinguished career.[39]

Insinuations of plagiarism also would have been a hard pill for Florence Price to swallow. Price, a freelance teacher, pianist, organist, and composer who had studied at the New England Conservatory between 1903 and 1906 (see figure 8.4), heard her First Symphony performed by Frederick Stock and the Chicago Symphony Orchestra in June 1933, just over a year before Dawson's. Echoing Dvořák, she said in one of her few written statements about musical style that "we are even beginning to believe in the possibility of establishing a national musical idiom," and "we are waking up to the fact that we *already* have a folk music in the Negro spirituals—music which is potent, poignant, compelling." Her First Symphony, which shares the E minor key with Dvořák's, exhibits melodic and rhythmic figures found in African-derived folk music and dance. Perhaps she was the composer Will Marion Cook had prophesied.[40]

FIGURE 8.4. Florence Price, ca. 1933. Courtesy Special Collections, University of Arkansas Libraries, Fayetteville.

"As we listened to that concert," Robert Abbot wrote in the *Chicago Defender* after hearing the symphony, "we took hope yet again that there may yet be brotherhood in this land of ours." On the previous evening—an "American Night" program—George—Gershwin performed his *Rhapsody in Blue* on a program that didn't feature a single Black performer or composer. Between 1893 and 1933, the inclusion of Black voices under the rubric of "American music" had evidently remained an open question. Price died in 1953, fifty-five years before the premiere of her Fourth Symphony, which conductor Artur Rodziński of the Cleveland Orchestra had refused to perform during her lifetime.

NOTES

1 "This is Progress," *ChiDef*, 24 June 1933.
2 See also Adrienne Fried Block, "Dvořák's Long American Reach," in *Dvořák in America*, ed. Tibbetts, 157–81.
3 Dvořák, "Music in America," *Harper's*, Feb. 1895, 429–34; "The New York Musical Society," *NYEP*, 6 May 1895.
4 "A Dvořák Society," *Colored American*, 20 Mar. 1900; Berenice Thompson, "Letter from Washington," *MC*. 6 June 1900, 11.
5 Russell, "The Great Dvořák Dead," *Indianapolis Freeman*, 4 June 1904.
6 Maude Cuney-Hare, *Negro Musicians and Their Music* (Washington, DC: Associated Publishers, 1936), 57–59; Eileen Southern, *The Music of Black Americans: A History*, 3rd ed. (New York: W. W. Norton, 1997), 266–69.
7 "Concerts and Lectures," *BDG*, 31 Dec. 1893.
8 "Seidl Society Concert," *BDE*, 12 Jan. 1894.
9 "Philharmonic Concerts," *MT* (July 1894): 460.
10 "Music at the Academy," *Philadelphia North American*, 23 Oct. 1894.
11 "Arias of a Republic," *ChiTr*, 4 Nov. 1894.
12 "Over Now," *CinCG*, 2 Jan. 1895.
13 "Concerte," *Neue Freie Presse*, 23 Feb. 1896 (my translation).
14 Concert program, 10 Nov 1907, Program ID 8182, New York Philharmonic Leon Levy Digital Archives.
15 "Dvořák in the New World," *NYS*, 1 Jan. 1911.
16 "Dvořák's New Symphony," *BDE*, 21 Dec. 1893.
17 "Music in Brooklyn," *BDE*, 1894; "Prof. Ellsworth C. Phelps," *NYS*, 1 Dec. 1913; Shadle, *Orchestrating the Nation*, 191–220.
18 "Organ Loft Whisperings," *MC*, 21 June 1893, 11; "Bristow's New Choral Symphony," *AAJ*, 6 June 1896, 130–31; "Music Teacher Dies in School," *NYS*, 14 Dec. 1898; Shadle, *Orchestrating the Nation*, 256–62.
19 "Cultivating the Negro Voice," *NYS*, 7 Jan. 1894; quoted in "The Negro in American Music," *Philadelphia Record*, 17 Feb. 1896.
20 "A Music School of High Ideals," *MA*, 31 Aug. 1912, 23; "Introduces Bill to Found National School of Music," *MA*, 27 Oct. 1917, 6; "Bill in Congress for Land Grant to Music School Arouses Protests," *MA*, 15 July 1922, 2; "Juilliard

Merger Details Announced," *MA*, 4 Dec. 1926, 2; Rubin, "Jeannette Meyers Thurber," 312–17.
21. "Just Two Letters," *New York Amsterdam News*, 5 Oct. 1927; Marva Carter, *Swing Along: The Musical Life of Will Marion Cook* (New York: Oxford University Press, 2008), 36–115.
22. Jean Snyder, *Harry T. Burleigh: From the Spiritual to the Harlem Renaissance* (Urbana: University of Illinois Press, 2016), 298–323; Christopher A. Brooks and Robert Sims, *Roland Hayes: The Legacy of an American Tenor* (Bloomington: Indiana University Press, 2014), 32–52.
23. Beckerman, *New Worlds*, 126–37; "Mephisto's Musings," *MA*, 25 Feb. 1939, 9; Jean Snyder, "A Great and Noble School of Music: Dvořák, Harry T. Burleigh, and the African American Spiritual," in *Dvořák in America*, ed. Tibbetts, 123–48.
24. "Sousa's Farewell Before World Tour," *MA*, 12 Nov. 1910, 32; Broekhoven, "The Alien Musician in America," *MO*, Nov. 1921, 25; "Creole Suite for Symphony Orchestra," *MO*, Nov. 1929, 62.
25. "Henry Schoenefeld," *Freund's Musical Weekly*, 22 Jan. 1896, 6; "Henry Schoenefeld," *Pacific Coast Musician*, 15 Aug. 1936, 9.
26. Gilbert, "A Chapter of Reminiscence," *NMR*, 21 Jan. 1921, 56.
27. "Objects of New Music Society," *MA*, 6 Jan 1906, 12; Gilbert, "A Chapter of Reminiscence," *NMR*, Feb. 1921, 94.
28. "American Works on Stransky Program," *MA*, 13 Dec. 1913, 41; Downes, "Olin Downes 'Hears America Singing' in Henry Gilbert's *Negro Rhapsody*," *MA*, 28 June 1913, 14.
29. Holt, "The Symphony Concert," *ChiDef*, 9 Mar. 1919.
30. Helen Walker-Hill, "Black Women Composers in Chicago: Then and Now," *Black Music Research Journal* 12 (1992): 9; Lucy Caplan, "'Strange What Cosmopolites Music Makes of Us': Classical Music, the Black Press, and Nora Douglas Holt's Black Feminist Audiotopia," *Journal of the Society for American Music* 14 (2020): 308–36.
31. Du Bois, "Strivings of the Negro People," *Atlantic Monthly*, Aug. 1897, 194–98; see Ernest Allen, Jr., "Du Boisian Double Consciousness: The Unsustainable Argument," *Massachusetts Review* 43 (2002): 217–53 and Wilson J. Moses, "W. E. B. Du Bois's 'The Conservation of Races' and Its Context: Idealism, Conservatism, and Hero Worship," *Massachusetts Review* 34 (1993): 275–94.
32. Sinclair to Du Bois, 2 Oct. 1914, DBP; Du Bois to Sinclair, 19 Oct. 1914, DBP; Anne Whitney Wakefield to Du Bois, 10 Aug. 1924, DBP; Du Bois to Wakefield, 7 Oct. 1924, DBP.
33. "Spirituals," *The Crisis*, Feb. 1927, 210–11.
34. Valentine to Du Bois, 25 Oct. 1926, DBP; Du Bois to Valentine, 3 Jan. 1926 [1927], DBP; Fisher to Du Bois, 26 Feb. 1927, DBP; "The Browsing Reader," *The Crisis*, Sep. 1927, 227–28.

35 "Powell's Creative Gifts Again Admired," *MA*, 30 Mar. 1918, 22.
36 Powell, "Music and the Nation," *Rice Institute Pamphlet* 10 (July 1923): 146–63; Jonathan Spiro, *Defending the Master Race: Conservation, Eugenics, and the Legacy of Madison Grant* (Lebanon, NH: University Press of New England, 2009), 254–58.
37 See Folder 15, LSP.
38 Evanti to Dawson, 16 Nov. 1934, WDP; White to Dawson, 13 Nov. 1934; WDP.
39 Alain Locke, *The Works of Alain Locke*, ed. Charles Molesworth (New York: Oxford University Press, 2012), 145; "Symphonic Novelties Brighten Orchestral Fortnight," *MA*, 16 Dec. 1934, 8; "Dawson Replies to His Accusers," *Pittsburgh Courier*, 24 Nov. 1934; see also Gwynne Kuhner Brown, "Whatever Happened to William Dawson's *Negro Folk Symphony*?," *Journal of the Society for American Music* 6 (2012): 433–56.
40 Box 1, Folder 3, FPPA; see also Samantha Ege, "Composing a Symphonist: Florence Price and the Hand of Black Women's Fellowship," *Women and Music* 24 (2020): 7–27.

EPILOGUE
THE GREAT BEYOND

On February 26, 2008, Loren Maazel and the New York Philharmonic performed for a packed East Pyongyang Grand Theater in North Korea. Chairman Kim Jong-il was conspicuously absent. The program included Gershwin's *American in Paris* and the prelude to Act III of Wagner's *Lohengrin*, as well as encores by Georges Bizet and Leonard Bernstein.

The centerpiece, however, was Dvořák's New World Symphony. Maazel introduced it to the audience by saying it contained a Native American folksong, while the program book claimed that "Dvořák always downplayed whatever debt to American music might lie in these much-admired pages." Which was it? Either way, the audience loved it.

"There's no question about it," Maazel told a reporter afterward. "If it does come to be seen in retrospect as a historical moment, we will all be very proud."[1]

Standard narratives about the New World Symphony's residual cultural impact have focused on the development of various musical styles—classical and commercial. Yet Dvořák's provocative statements about style appeared in the very same article in which the National Conservatory made the even more radical announcement that it would admit Black students free of charge. As director, Dvořák envisioned a world in which students could pursue whatever their musical ambitions might be. But what he found and left behind was a classical music industry actively hostile to all people of African descent—composers, performers, and even audiences. After facing rejection from white classical institutions, countless Black musicians chose to enter the commercial industry, which was also notoriously exploitative, teach or study in Black schools and churches, or forsake professional musicianship altogether. Meanwhile, white American composers complained bitterly about their own lack of opportunity.

The standard narratives contain grains of truth, but they need to account for the significant realities they overlook: the experiences of aspiring Black classical musicians. Gamewell Valentine of Sumter, South Carolina, whom I introduced in chapter 8, wrote W. E. B. Du Bois again in 1930 to ask for advice. He explained that he'd lived in New York for a while as a teenager, and had even been accepted to the Clef Club, but returned home after his mother begged him. He then studied music for a time at Morehouse College in Atlanta, where he met Black luminaries like Marian Anderson and Clarence Cameron White. Wilbur Thirkield, president of Howard University, offered him a scholarship to finish his training there, but he couldn't afford to live in Washington. Instead he stayed in South Carolina, where he led community music programs in Greenville and taught in several schools, all with great success. But, he wrote,

> I am cramped, cramped in South Carolina. No contact; no inspiration; no opportunity for further self-development; no encouragement; "no nothing." [. . .] My wife and I have talked it over. She wants me to come to New York to study, to take a chance, to see if success would be within reach. I feel the urge to come now or never. We have arranged for her and my boy's welfare while I come to New York. I make no satisfactory headway in the South. I have almost buried my talent and ability. My enthusiasm has been deadened.[2]

He asked Du Bois if he should do it. And Du Bois told him the truth: "The conventional and proper answer to anyone who contemplates coming to New York is don't do it." But he offered the names of two contacts—composers Carl Diton and Jeannette Norman—and apologized that he couldn't be more encouraging. This anxious struggle was real life for Valentine and any number of Black musicians facing uncertain futures.[3]

At the same time, Black classical musicians created ways to thrive despite the challenges posed by predominantly white organizations. Black women's music clubs and the National Association of Negro Musicians became vital networks for supporting composition, performance, and musical community. Harriet Gibbs Marshall's Washington Conservatory of Music, founded in 1903, educated generations of Black musicians and enhanced the city's vibrant musical life until it closed in 1960. During the New Deal era, Black ensembles sponsored by the Federal Music Project became staples of local music scenes throughout the country. And white conductors like Frederick Stock and Leopold Stokowski programmed Black composers even though the decision came with a degree of professional risk. Valentine didn't necessarily need to go to New York to find what he was seeking. He needed the types of support that white musicians could take for granted, even when they were down on their luck.[4]

Coincidentally, I finished this book just as the country grieved the brutal murder of George Floyd—a contemporary police lynching on display for the entire world to see. Writer Ta-Nehisi Coates noted in his reflections on Ezra Edelman's documentary about O. J. Simpson that the legacy of police brutality in this country, which extends backward far beyond the Jim Crow era and into antebellum slave patrols, shaped the jury's decision to acquit Simpson. "He'd gotten away with it," Coates observed, "in much the same way that white people had killed Black men and women for centuries and gotten away with it."[5]

With this backdrop, I find it impossible to think of the New World Symphony as a symbol of international cooperation and goodwill, as Loren Maazel would have it. The stories captured in this book compel me to hear the symphony as a musical crystallization of fraught American race relations. The piece exposed the deep wounds of racism and continued to poke at them for decades, often by emboldening white racists to continue antagonizing Black music and musicians. Even so, great Black American conductors of the twentieth century, such as Everett Lee, Dean Dixon, and James DePreist, made it a staple of their own portfolios, claiming it as part of an American musical inheritance. Perhaps the next time we think about listening to it, or programming it, we might remember the musical sounds Dvořák himself wanted to hear after he landed on American shores—the sounds of Black music and musicians—and ensure our ears can hear them, too.

NOTES

1. Daniel Wakin, "At Landmark Pyongyang Concert, 'My Heart is Booming,'" *International Herald Tribune*, 27 Feb. 2008.
2. Valentine to Du Bois, 4 July 1930, DBP.
3. Du Bois to Valentine, 14 July 1930, DBP.
4. See Doris Evans McGinty, "'As Large as She Can Make It': The Role of Black Women Activists in Music, 1880–1945," in *Cultivating Music in America: Women Patrons and Activists Since 1860*, ed. Ralph P. Locke and Cyrilla Barr (Berkeley: University of California Press, 1997), 214–36; Kenneth J. Bandas, *All of This Music Belongs to the Nation: The WPA's Federal Music Project and American Society* (Knoxville: University of Tennessee Press, 1995), 71–85.
5. Ta-Nehisi Coates, "What O. J. Simpson Means to Me," *The Atlantic*, Oct. 2016, 87.

APPENDIX
THE MUSICAL TORNADO

As news of Dvořák's midwestern travels circulated through the press in late spring 1893, John P. Jackson, music critic for the *New York Recorder*, wondered how the sounds Dvořák might encounter there might affect his theories about an American classical style. According to an obituary in the *Musical Courier*, Jackson was "the most unswerving, even fanatical, admirer of Wagner's music" and a "close personal friend of the great composer." This parody, which the *Courier* reprinted from the *Recorder* on June 7, deftly captured the nexus of aesthetics, national identity, and racism found in the heated discussions about Dvořák's music and ideas that raged in the press throughout 1893 and 1894. I include it here to capture the flavor of writing that permeated through music criticism of the era.[1]

DVOŘÁK AND THE NATIONAL TORNADO

We have a great musical genius dwelling among us. He was imported for the purpose of implanting upon one of our great conservatories the seeds of America's future greatness in the musical world. Antonín Dvořák came to us from Bohemia, a country which Shakespeare declared had a seaport, and which some of our worthy musical leaders have told us has produced in Antonín a bigger man than Wagner.

Antonín has given us a few real surprises during the last few weeks. Instead of asserting that European musical culture should be fed to our young musical world, he suddenly discovered that we possess a marvelous musical bonanza in our negro melodies, and told us that instead of wasting time in studying Beethoven, Wagner, Mozart or even Dvořák our national music should be built upon and developed from the melodies of the dusky African, who came here originally with his tom-toms from the fever stricken coast of Guinea and the Congo, but in some mysterious way won during his slavery years the original melodies of mysterious Nature from the whisperings of the cotton bale and the canebrake.

Many great European musicians have undoubtedly built up their great reputations on worse materials. Dvořák himself has dished up his own country's national dances most successfully, just as Brahms, Liszt, Moszkowski, and others have done with theirs. But negro melodies, as the foundation of the American school of music of the future, pale into insignificance in the face of the possibilities now hinted at by Mr. Dvořák. The great Bohemian still intends to gather his inspiration from purely American sources, but if we are to believe current stories he has the heroic intention of making a musical pilgrimage to Minnesota for the purpose of listening to the giant melodies of the cyclone, to digest them on the spot, and finally to incorporate them into a great American national symphony poem, to which the storm in Beethoven's Pastoral Symphony and the wild rush of the Valkyries' Ride will be as gentle summer zephyrs.

Our distinguished Bohemian maestro has undoubtedly taken upon himself a great contract. We can already hear the great symphonic poem in imagination—the quiet peacefulness of the plains, the rustle of the broad fields of ripening grain, the sharp click of the harvesting machines—the sudden silence, the gathering of the storm, the scurrying of the people to find shelter in their cyclone caves—then chaos itself, the swooping rush and roar of the elements, the crash of houses, intermingled with the cries of anguish of the farmyard animals and babies in their cradles, all whirled round and round and upward by the demonical powers and taken to eternity. The silence, and, instead of the rustic dance of old-fashioned European composers, negro melodies, "Push Dem Clouds Away" and "Climbing up the Golden Stairs," wafted from the sunny South, and a gorgeous finale in which "The Star Spangled Banner," in polyphonic beauty of orchestration, shall close the great American masterpiece. What a subject for American music of the future!

We expect great things from Mr. Dvořák when he emerges from his cyclone cave with all these ideas ready to be put into American musical language of the future.

We sincerely trust that our great Bohemian maestro will be able to give the diabolical grandeur of the scene he promises musically to depict without endangering his life or depriving our younger generation of students of the benefits of European musical culture which he brought over with him. But we can hardly see how Mr. Dvořák is to get the necessary cyclonic inspiration for his symphonic poem if he hides himself away in a cyclonic cave while the terrible storm is raging without. And if our great maestro ventures to remain outside, instead of getting into the sheltering cave, we are sadly afraid that, though he may get the necessary cyclonic inspiration for his work, we shall have no grand resulting national American symphonic poem of Mr. Dvořák, who, brought here to impart to us the benefits of European musical culture, found, while trying to wrest the secrets of diabolical musical beauty from the aboriginal and unchained elements of our great West, a noble and heroic death.

NOTE

1 "Raconteur," *MC*, 8 Dec. 1897, 23.

SUGGESTED READING

Accessible literature on the topics covered in this book is vast. Beginning with broad histories: Nell Irvin Painter's sweeping *History of White People* is essential reading on the construction of whiteness as a racial concept. Matthew Frye Jacobson's *Whiteness of a Different Color* zooms in on the post-Reconstruction era and the question of racial assimilation. Henry Louis Gates Jr.'s *Stony the Road* deftly frames the challenges faced by Black Americans at the dawn of the Jim Crow era. Daniel Sharfstein's bracing *Thunder in the Mountains* explores the complex and often brutal government interventions into the lives of Black Americans and Native Americans during the same period, while Edlie Wong's *Racial Reconstruction* examines similar dynamics between Chinese Americans and Black Americans.

Several books equipped me with valuable tools for seeing "the Dvořák moment" through the lens of race. Eileen Southern's monumental *The Music of Black Americans* is essential for understanding the core narratives underpinning Black American musicmaking. Ronald Radano's *Lying Up a Nation* and Guthrie Ramsey Jr.'s *Race Music* offer critical perspectives on the historical construction of Black musical identities. And although I did not treat the issue of Asian American musical identities in depth here, Deborah Wong's *Speak It Louder* is required reading for broader context.

Michael Beckerman's *New Worlds of Dvořák* offers indispensable insight into the composer's US residency and its effects on his life and music. It is my top recommendation for further reading on the New World Symphony specifically. E. Douglas Bomberger's *"A Tidal Wave of Encouragement"* explores the push to introduce American composers to audiences in the United States and Europe during the second half of the nineteenth century.

Stellar biographies of relevant musicians include Rae Linda Brown on Florence Price, Jean E. Snyder on Harry T. Burleigh, Marva Griffin Carter on Will Marion Cook, and Katherine K. Preston on George Frederick Bristow. Sandra Jean Graham's *Spirituals and the Birth of a Black Entertainment Industry* and *Out of Sight* by Lynn Abbott and Doug Seroff offer richly detailed accounts of African American involvement in the era's commercial music industry, while Jon Michael Spencer's *The New Negroes and Their Music* provides an invaluable exposition of classical music's relationship to the Harlem Renaissance.

Finally, several authors have tackled questions about Native American musical practices and classical music in far greater depth than I have here: John Troutman in *Indian Blues*, Beth E. Levy in *Frontier Figures*, and Michael V. Pisani in *Imagining Native America in Music*.

INDEX

For the benefit of digital users, indexed terms that span two pages (e.g., 52–53) may, on occasion, appear on only one of those pages.

Tables, figures and boxes are indicated by *t*, *f* and *b* following the page number

Abbot, Robert, 138, 159
absolute music, 41–44, 49–50, 55
abstract instrumental music, 42
Altschuler, Modest, 155
Ambros, August Wilhelm, 46–47
American national style, 57–60. *See also* national musical identity
  and compositional technique before Dvořák's arrival, 94–97
  and critical reception of New World Symphony, 129–34
  Dvořák and, 76–77
  Dvořák clarifies ideas about, 107–9
  Dvořák's interview on, 97–100
  endorsed by European luminaries, 84–88
  folk music and, 74–75
  impact of Dvořák's midwestern travels on, 171–74
  international reactions to Dvořák's interview on, 100–7
  Krehbiel on, 75–76
  racial politics and Dvořák's views on, 122–25
  rooted in Black vernacular music, 84–88
American Negro Academy, 153
American Opera Company, 5–6, 7
American Opera School, 5–12
anti-Czech sentiment, 60
Arens, Franz Xavier, 73*b*–74, 85–87, 86*f*, 88, 151
Arnold, Maurice, 92, 97
art music
  origins of, 57
  in United States, 57–60

Beach, Amy, 104
Bennett, James, 62–63
Bird, Arthur, 106–7
Black classical musicians, 140, 166–68
Black music students, 34, 119–22, 124, 140, 144–45, 166–67
Black vernacular music
  and critical reception of New World Symphony, 127, 128, 129–34
  Douglass on, 153–55

Black vernacular music (*cont.*)
  Dvořák clarifies ideas about American national style and, 107–9
  Dvořák supports style rooted in, 97–100, 122–25
  exploitation of, 57–58
  Florence Price and, 159–61
  Harry T. Burleigh and, 146–47
  Henry F. Gilbert and, 148–52
  Henry Schoenefeld and, 148
  and impact of New World Symphony, 139–41
  international reaction to Dvořák's support for style rooted in, 100–7
  John Broekhoven and, 147–48
  John W. Powell and, 155–56
  Lamar Stringfield and, 156–57
  as source of compositional inspiration, 34–35, 75, 78–84
  William Dawson and, 157–59
  Will Marion Cook and, 146
Blaine, James, 3–5
Bolin, Gaius C., 119–21
Bolin, Paul, 117–20
Bonds, Margaret, 138
Boston *Musical Herald*, Dvořák's interview with, 98–101
Bouhy, Jacques, 8
Braham, David, 103
Brahms, Johannes, 19–20, 24, 25*t*
  Symphony No. 3, 27–28
Bristow, George Frederick, 58–59, 143–44
Broekhoven, John, 81*f*, 85
  Suite Creole, 80–82, 147–50
Bruckner, Anton, 100–1
Burleigh, Harry T., 34, 92, 97, 117–20, 125, 146–47
Busoni, Ferruccio, 39, 40

Cable, George Washington, 80
Cable, George William, 148–50

Carnegie's Music Hall, 12, 15*b*–17*b*, 117–19
Cincinnati May Festival (1884), 63–65
Claus, J. B., 102
Coates, Ta-Nehisi, 168
colonialism, national musical identity and, 55–56
Comedy Overture (Gilbert), 151–52
Cook, Will Marion, 116–19, 117*f*, 125, 133–34, 146
Corder, Frederick, 62, 66–67, 68–69
Cornelius, Peter, 43–44
cosmopolitanism, 33, 65, 67–68
Cowen, Frederic Hymen, 24, 27, 30, 66
  "Welsh" symphony, 66
Craig, Walter F., 119–20
Creelman, James, 99–101
Crinkle, Nym, 130
Cuney-Hare, Maud, 140–41

Damrosch, Leopold, 19, 21*f*, 24
Damrosch, Walter, 21*f*, 127–28
Dawson, William, 158*f*
  Negro Folk Symphony, 157–59
Debussy, Claude, 83–84
De Koven, Reginald, 104, 127
DePreist, James, 168–69
Dixon, Dean, 168–69
Douglass, Frederick, 113–14, 116, 117–19, 153
Downes, Olin, 151
Du Bois, W. E. B., 153–55, 166–67
Dunbar, Paul Laurence, 146, 153
Dvořák, Antonín. See also *Symphony No. 9, "From the New World"* (Dvořák)
  activities following New World Symphony premiere, 139
  and admission of Black students to National Conservatory, 121–22
  background of, 17–19
  on Black voice students, 144–45
  clarifies ideas about American national style, 107–9

commercial reach and longevity
    of, 28–31
competition of, 17b, 24, 25t, 27
compositional dexterity of, 68
considered for American Opera
    School, 30–31
directs National Conservatory's student charity concert, 91–93
as influence on American
    music, 76–77
international reaction to support of,
    for style rooted in Black vernacular music, 100–7
interview with Boston *Musical
    Herald,* 98–101
midwestern travels and theories
    about American classical style
    of, 171–74
"negro melodies" as influence
    on, 78–84
and premiere of New World
    Symphony, 125–29
Requiem, 31–32
residency at National
    Conservatory, 31–35
rise to popularity in United
    States, 17–24
signs on with American Opera
    School, 10–12
Stabat Mater, 29
supports style rooted in Black vernacular music, 97–100, 122–25
as symphonist of future, 67–69
Symphony No. 5, 28–29
Symphony No. 6, 24, 28–29,
    48–50, 59, 60
Symphony No. 7, 27, 28–29,
    49–50, 62–63
Symphony No. 8, 32–33, 67–68
Dvořák Musical Society, 140
Dwight, John Sullivan, 42, 44, 46, 95

"Eastern European" orchestral music,
    21–23, 22t

East Pyongyang Grand Theater, 165–66
economic hardship, 121–22
Edelman, Ezra, 168
Elson, Louis, 104
"Emancipation Symphony"
    (Phelps), 79–80
European imperialism, national musical identity and, 55–56
Evanti, Lillian, 157

Fay, Amy, 79
Fenner, Thomas P., 124–25
Finck, Henry, 27–28, 31–32, 50, 66,
    67–68, 139
Fischer, J., 147–48
Fisher, William Arms, 147, 154–55
Fisk Jubilee Singers, 122–23
Floyd, George, 168
folksongs and folk music, 56–57, 59,
    66–67, 69, 74–75
Foster, Stephen, 57–58, 109
Fry, William Henry, 58
    *Santa Claus: Christmas
    Symphony,* 42–43

German national sentiment and identity, 60–61, 63–67
Gershwin, George, 137, 159
Gesamtkunstwerk, 46
Gilbert, Henry F., 148–52, 150f
Gilchrist, William Wallace, 96
Gleason, Frederic Grant, 96
Goldmark, Rubin, 106
Goodrich, A. J., 87–88, 122, 131–32
Gottschalk, Louis Moreau, 78–79,
    85, 87–88
Great Britain, Dvořák's reputation
    in, 29–30

Hale, Philip, 142–43
Hanslick, Eduard, 43–44, 60, 142
Harrigan, Ed, 103
Harris, William Torrey, 9
Hassard, John, 19, 21–23, 24, 48–49

Hayes, Roland, 137–38, 146–47
Hayson, Walter B., 124, 132–33, 153
Hearn, Lafcadio, 80
Heinrich, Anthony Philip, 42, 58
Henderson, W. J., 2, 27–29, 31–32, 129–30
Higginson, Henry Lee, 6
Higginson, Thomas Wentworth, 2, 97
higher education, evolution of, 3
Holt, Lena James, 152
Huneker, James, 27–28, 97, 98, 130–31, 132

imperialism, national musical identity and, 55–56

Jackson, John P., 171–74
Joachim, Joseph, 100–1
Johnson, James Weldon, 147
Jones, Sissieretta, 91, 109, 116–17, 118*f*, 119

Klänge aus Amerika (Saddler), 83*f*, 84–85
Král, Josef Jiří, 125–26
Krehbiel, Henry
   on American national music, 75–76
   and Broekhoven's *Suite Creole*, 80
   and change in New York's critical makeup, 27–28
   on Dvořák as American Opera School director, 31
   on Dvořák's compositional ascendancy, 68–69
   on European reception of American compositions, 87
   as influence on Dvořák, 98
   and national musical identity, 63–67
   on Requiem, 31–32
   on Symphony No. 5, 28–29
   on Symphony No. 7, 27, 49–50
   on Symphony No. 9, 41, 69, 128–29
   writes on New World Symphony, 16*b*

Lavallée, Calixa, 58–59
Lee, Everett, 168–69
Levi, Hermann, 85
Lewis, J. Henry, 140
Liebling, Sally, 100–1
Listemann, Bernhard, 19
Liszt, Franz, 43–46
   Les préludes, 44
Locke, Alain, 157
Longfellow, Henry, *Song of Hiawatha*, 34, 126
Lothian, Napier, 102
Lyric Swan Club, 5

Maas, Louis, 58–59
Maazel, Loren, 165–66
MacDowell, Edward, 96, 148–50
Mandyczewski, Eusebius, 100–1
Manoury, Théophile-Adolphe, 8
Margulies, Adele, 10–11
Marshall, Harriet Gibbs, 144–45, 167–68
Marteau, Henri, 15*b*
Mason, William, 44
Mees, Arthur, 40, 50, 54–55
Mendelssohn School of Music, 5
Metropolitan Opera House, 11–12
Mollenhauer, William, 104–5
music
   debates on nature of, 41–46, 104–5
   expressive universality of, 95–96, 104–5
musical education
   Black Americans' access to, 119–22, 123–24, 144–45, 166–67
   evolution of, 3–6

National Conservatory, 30–31, 33, 84, 91–93, 119–22, 144–45, 166
nationalism, 105
national musical identity, 55–57. *See also* American national style; German national sentiment and identity

of Dvořák works, 60–63
German, 60–63
Krehbiel and, 63–67
in United States, 57–60
Native American melodies, 126, 128
Negro Folk Symphony (Dawson), 157–59
"negro melodies." *See* Black vernacular music
Negro Rhapsody (Gilbert), 151
New Music Society, 150–51, 155
New World Symphony. See *Symphony No. 9, "From the New World"* (Dvořák)
New York Recorder, 171–74
"Niagara" (Bristow), 144
Niagara Symphony (Fry), 58
North Korea, New World Symphony performed in, 165–66

Ornithological Combat of Kings, The (Heinrich), 58
Osgood, George, 105–6

Paine, John Knowles, 24, 46–47, 58–59, 105
Paur, Emil, 145
Pearce, G. Wilfred, 132, 133
Perkins, Charles Callahan, 46
Peyser, Herbert, 155–56
Phelps, Ellsworth, 79–80, 143–44
police brutality, 168
poverty, 121–22
Powell, John W., 8–9, 155–56
  Rhapsodie nègre, 155–56
Les préludes (Liszt), 44
Price, Florence, 138, 159–61

racial politics
  and Cook opera based on *Uncle Tom's Cabin,* 116–19, 125
  and critical reception of New World Symphony, 129–34
  and Dvořák's views on American musical style, 122–25

National Conservatory and, 119–22
and New World Symphony as crystallization of fraught American race relations, 168–69
and premiere of New World Symphony, 125–29
and World's Columbian Exposition, 113–16
Raff, Joachim, 47–48
Rathbun, F. G., 124–25
Requiem (Dvořák), 31–32
Reyer, Ernest, 100–1
Rhapsodie nègre (Powell), 155–56
Richter, Hans, 30, 60, 100–1
"Ride of the Valkyries" (Wagner), 47
Rogers, Philip Clayton, 102
Rubinstein, Anton, 47–48, 74*b*, 88, 100–1, 106–7
Russell, Sylvester, 140

Saddler, Frank E., *Klänge aus Amerika,* 83*f*, 84–85
Safonov, Vasily, 145
Santa Claus: Christmas Symphony (Fry), 42–43
Schirmer, Gustav, 19–20
Schoenefeld, Henry, 73*b*–74*b*, 82, 85–87, 88, 98, 106–7, 148
scientific music, 56–57
Scoville, Charles, 85
Seidl, Anton, 15*b*, 16*b*–17*b*, 39–40, 44–46, 53, 108–9
Simpson, O. J., 168
Simrock, Fritz, 19–20
Sinclair, Upton, 153–54
slavery, 57–58, 79–80, 87–88, 101–2, 122–23, 125–26, 130, 131–32, 140, 153–54. *See also* Black vernacular music
Slavonic orchestral music, 21–23, 22*t*
Smith, Harry, 34, 122–23
Song of Hiawatha (Longfellow), 34, 126
Sousa, John Philip, 147–48
Southern, Eileen, 140–41

Stabat Mater (Dvořák), 29
Steinberg, Albert, 66, 128–29
Stock, Frederick, 137–38
Stringfield, Lamar, 156–57
Suite Creole (Broekhoven), 80–82, 147–50
symphony, as German genre, 60–63, 65–66
Symphony No. 3 (Brahms), 27–28
Symphony No. 4 (Cowan), 27
Symphony No. 5 (Dvořák), 28–29
Symphony No. 6 (Dvořák), 24, 28–29, 48–50, 59, 60
Symphony No. 7 (Dvořák), 27, 28–29, 49–50, 62–63
Symphony No. 8 (Dvořák), 32–33, 67–68
Symphony No. 9, "From the New World" (Dvořák)
  background of, 31–35
  continued responses to, 141–42
  critical responses to, 126–34
  as crystallization of fraught American race relations, 168–69
  and debates concerning national musical identity, 55
  description of premiere of, 15b–17b, 39–41, 53–55
  following Dvořák's death, 142–43
  impact of, 137–39
  impact of, in Black musical circles, 139–41
  influence of nonwhite sources on, 34–35
  performed in North Korea, 165–66
  Phelps and Bristow's accusation concerning, 143–44
  premiere of, 125–29
  program for premiere of, 18f
  residual cultural impact of, 166–67

Tchaikovsky, Piotr Ilyich, 30
Thirkield, Wilbur, 166–67
Thomas, Theodore, 5–6, 7, 19, 24, 47, 55, 82
Thompson, A., 107
Thoms, William, 49, 59, 78, 87–88
Thurber, Jeannette, 3, 4f, 5–12, 30–31, 33–34, 117–20, 144–45
Thurman, Allen, 3–5
Trenkler, August, 73b
Trotter, James Monroe, 123

Uncle Tom's Cabin (Stowe), opera based on, 116–19, 125, 134
universalism, 95–96, 104–5

Valentine, Gamewell, 154–55, 166–67
Van Cleve, John, 47, 82

Wagner, Richard, 42, 46–48, 171
  "Ride of the Valkyries," 47
Wagnerism, criticism of Dvořák in relation to, 48–50
Walker, Fanny Payne, 119
Warren, Richard Henry, 1–2
Washington Conservatory of Music, 167–68
Watson, Henry Cood, 78
Wells, Ida B., 116
"Welsh" symphony (Cowen), 66
White, Clarence Cameron, 157
White, Richard Grant, 47
Whiting, George E., 79, 106–7
Willis, Richard Storrs, 42–43
Wilson, George H., 87, 95
World's Columbian Exposition (Chicago, 1893), 113–16

Ysaÿe, Eugène, 53, 54

www.ingramcontent.com/pod-product-compliance
Ingram Content Group UK Ltd.
Pitfield, Milton Keynes, MK11 3LW, UK
UKHW020651201025
464067UK00019B/136